Mainlining Philly

Mainlining Philly

SURVIVAL, HOPE,
AND RESISTING
DRUG ADDICTION

Geri-Lynn Utter, PsyD.

Literary House Publishers
https://literaryhousepublishers.com

Ordering Information:
Quantity sales. Special discounts are available on quantity purchases by
corporations, associations, and others. For details, contact the publisher at the web address above.

Printed in the United States of America

Library of Congress Control Number: 2020911334

Publisher's Cataloging-in-Publication data

Utter, Geri-Lynn.
Mainlining Philly: Survival, Hope, and Resisting
Drug Addiction/ Geri-Lynn Utter

ISBN 978-0-578-71314-4

First Edition

CONTENTS

INTRODUCTION

WHY THIS BOOK?

Unlike most other books about addiction, this book offers both a professional and a personal perspective on the subject. I am considered an expert in the field of addiction not only because of my education and clinical experience (I am a Psy.D. clinical psychologist), but also because both my parents are drug addicts. I'm a witness to countless addicts who lived and died in my parents' wildly dysfunctional and often blatantly criminal inner circle during my childhood in one of the roughest areas of Philadelphia.

Long before I cracked open a book on the subject, my view of addiction was formed by witnessing its effects on real people. The familial and personal challenges I was confronted with during my youth helped me become a clinician with rare, real-world insight into addiction. More importantly, these challenges helped me develop genuine empathy for people gripped by addiction. Without being empathetic for those we treat, we can never really make a difference in helping addicts address this problem.

Believe me, it's easy to grow to hate a loved one who is in active addiction. It's as though the person you once knew no longer exists or that their physical body has been possessed by a demonic presence. But, as a society, when we begin to perceive drug addiction as the neurobiological, midbrain disease that it is rather than simply blaming it on the individual's moral failure or lack of willpower, we are creating a genuine opportunity for recovery among those struggling with this disease as we ease the burden of those who care for them.

My perspective arises from having been the child of addicted parents and from how their substance abuse and alcoholism (coupled, as these issues usually are, with severe mental health issues) influenced me to become a voice for others who are like my parents. In writing this book, I want my story to comfort people whose loved ones suffer from this disease. Although my personal experience with addiction, through my parents and their friends, was challenging and risky, it was a driving force in my desire to educate and inspire healthcare professionals, law enforcement personnel, and the general population about the disease of addiction.

There is often a trajectory for people suffering from opioid use disorder (OUD); they tend to start by using pain medications, such as Oxycontin or Percocet, before transitioning to heroin. Throughout my practice, I have heard many scenarios in which patients reported becoming addicted to pain medications for a multitude of reasons (chronic back pain, post-surgical pain, work- or accident-related injuries, etc.)

Before they realize it, their medication use has spiraled out of control. Consider the following example: A patient is prescribed a pain medication that he or she soon begins to take more frequently than prescribed. Eventually, he or she runs out of the medication before it is time for a refill and experiences acute withdrawal symptoms, such as abdominal cramping, diarrhea, sweating, body aches, insomnia, and irritability. In these instances, some patients manage to procure an additional prescription from their doctor, often by lying or manipulation (in most cases, physicians will not refill a narcotic prescription such as Percocet prior to its actual refill date).

Becoming dependent on and addicted to opioid pain medication can happen so quickly that by the time the patient begins to question the dangerous pattern of their abuse, it's often too late. Therefore, people who become addicted to initially prescribed opioids often begin to seek out non-prescribed opioid pain medication in order to support their addiction.

Buying illegal opioid pain medication is costly. For example, one 80 mg Oxycontin tablet is valued at around $20 on the street, depending on geographical and supply/demand factors. People who are addicted to pain medication may spend anywhere from $200 to $300 per day to support their habit, making it financially unsustainable. Due to these financial and access challenges, people who are actively abusing large quantities of pain medication may unexpectedly find themselves purchasing heroin.

Heroin is typically sold for $10 per bag on the East Coast. When an addict makes the transition from prescription pain medication to heroin, they can attain a high for a fraction of what they were paying for the pain medication; they can get the same high from a bag of heroin as they can get from 10 pills valued at approximately $200. Then, as the person builds a tolerance to heroin, they begin to need more and spend more. In a few months, they may go from using two bags of heroin daily to using a "bundle" — a slang term for 13 bags of heroin purchased at one time — and still spend less to support their heroin addiction than they would for a pain medication addiction.

Keep in mind that as a person's tolerance to heroin increases, their compulsion to use more also increases. It's at this juncture in the cycle of addiction when loved ones begin to notice behaviors in the addict that may be otherwise out of character for them, such as stealing, lying, or manipulating to obtain money in order to support the addiction.

For those of you who live with an addict, I want you to know that you can survive this with your mind and soul intact. For those of you who treat addicts, there is hope.

This is my story.

CHAPTER ONE

MY CRAZY BEGINNINGS

A Unique Past

I was born in Meadowbrook, Pennsylvania—a stone's throw from Philadelphia.

My parents married in 1975, but I wasn't conceived until five years later. According to my mother, she had spent a lot of that time convincing my father he was mature enough to become a father. He felt unprepared to raise a child because he had grown up in a wildly dysfunctional family and, in all truth, could barely take care of himself.

My mother, however, came from a traditional Italian-American family. And if you know anything about traditional Italian-American families, they expect daughters to give birth.

When my mother finally found herself with child, she wanted to name her after her dad, whose name was Jerome. Because everyone called him Jerry, she decided on the name Geri-Lynn.

That's how I got my name.

Yet, despite Dad's insistence that he wasn't suitable parent material, I wasn't my father's first child. Before marrying my mother in 1975, my father had dated two other women. One of them got pregnant and gave birth to my half-sister Denise. I believe his reluctance to become a father again was partially the result of his realization that he was negligently absent from Denise's life, having married my mother instead.

Also, according to my mother, my father cheated on her constantly while they were married; he was a very charismatic, good-looking man who had been a singer in a popular band, and he took advantage of that with the ladies. So that may have explained part of his reluctance to have another child.

But there was something even more important in my father's life than me, Denise, my mother, his music, or his other women.

Drugs.

My Father and Drugs

For the first three years of my life, my parents and I remained in the Meadowbrook area. My mother worked as a hairdresser. My father worked for Mrs. Smith's Pie Company.

Working a normal job must've been difficult for him. After all, he'd already enjoyed a successful singing career as a bass-baritone in the late 1960s. With his R&B group The Destinations, he even had a hit song on the soul music charts in the Philadelphia area. I believe it was at this time—during the anything-goes, drug-fueled 60s—that he started using illegal drugs, including heroin.

And shortly after I was born, he also turned to selling those drugs.

Like the people of all major cities, Philadelphians had a big appetite for marijuana, cocaine, and methamphetamine, especially in the early 1980s. My father, always looking for a way to make a buck, went into the business of satisfying that appetite.

He and my Uncle Cholly (short for Charlie) were in cahoots to distribute methamphetamine, even though the two didn't get along well. My uncle, a Vietnam veteran, had also become involved in drugs during the swinging 60s after returning home from the war. He was living in Kensington—an area of Philadelphia also known as "the Badlands." It was an area that would later become a significant part of my family's wild life.

To complicate matters, my father also began using methamphetamine, thus violating the dealer's rule, "never get high on your own supply."

Marge, Cholly's wife, was also involved in the illegal drug trade. She worked for my uncle and my father. I remember Marge well, mostly because she was such a tough customer. She brawled with grown men. She had been stabbed and shot by her previous husband. She and my uncle had two daughters, close to my age, named Ronni and Amber.

It was all unsustainable, and there was only one possible outcome. When I was four years old, my father was arrested for possession with intent to distribute. He was found guilty and sentenced to prison.

That's when my mother moved us into my grandmother's house in the Germantown section of Philadelphia. It's a historically Italian neighborhood that, by this time, had become largely African American. Around this time, my mother began to drink heavily. She and my grandmother would often fight. Though I was very young, I remember those battles well. Those types of memories never leave you.

While incarcerated, my father attempted to have my mother run his drug business. It wasn't much different from a legitimate business in that sense. He encouraged her to contact his young associate, Eddie, so everything could continue while he did his time. My mother and Eddie hit it off well. You could say a little too well, because my mother started a torrid affair with him that would stretch out across her entire life.

And Eddie would play a large, horrible role in my life.

Eddie

Eddie can be described in three words: dark, moody, and violent.

In his early twenties, Eddie was difficult when he was drinking alcohol. But he grew downright horrific when he was abusing Valium. The violence, the aggression he turned toward my mother at these times was awful.

Eddie's father was a Philadelphia police officer who was a raging alcoholic, and his mother was very submissive to whatever Eddie's father wanted. Eddie was one of four siblings, and he received the brunt of the severe physical abuse that his father delivered. As a result of prolonged physical abuse in conjunction with verbal abuse, Eddie turned to alcohol and also turned into his father.

My grandmother had had enough of Eddie, and she kicked my mother and me out of her home. I wasn't old enough to know all the particulars, but it must've been a tough decision for my mommom to make.

That's how, as a young child, I found myself roaming the streets with my mom and her new younger boyfriend, homeless. I remember hitching rides with my mother from strangers. I remember us asking people for money. I remember sleeping at many houses—friends, family, strangers.

I'm sure there is a lot I don't remember. One thing I do remember is being scared to death of Eddie. And that never changed once across the course of my life. In fact, I grew so uncomfortable with him that one day we reached the breaking point. The three of us were roaming the streets, the pavement hard under my little shoes. My mother was high on Valium. I don't remember what led me to make this decision, but I tried to run away.

I didn't get far. I remember Eddie running up behind me and knocking me to the ground, splitting my lip on the pavement. I cried for my father and prayed for rescue. But this was my life at that time; I had no say in it.

On another occasion, I remember my mother and Eddie dropping me off at a stranger's house. I did not know the people in the house, and I have no memory of them today. I must have been asleep when they dropped me off because when I awoke, I found myself alone in an unfamiliar dark room. It was quiet in the strange house, but I could hear someone snoring down the hall. I was scared, and even worse, I had to use the bathroom desperately. But I didn't know where it was located, and I was afraid to draw attention to myself by creeping around. At last, I couldn't hold my bladder any longer. Not knowing what else to do, I urinated in my pants.

Then I lay there on the sofa, staring up into the darkness, as the wet liquid cooled on my legs and bottom. I was four years old.

During that time, I felt anxious even when around my mother, and now, as an adult, I still do. The reason is simple: I have never felt safe around or protected by her. She didn't make sure that my basic needs were met. I never knew if we were going to have enough food, where we would be sleeping. That's why, later on, I took on the role of being both my mother's protector and caregiver.

But I had to raise myself first.

My Aunt Theresa

I will say this about my father: unlike my mother, he had a desire to protect me, even when he was in prison.

When he learned that my mother had spiraled into a state of semi-homelessness and substance abuse, he knew that he had to help me. From prison, my father contacted my aunt Theresa. He asked her if she would take me, her young niece, into her home. Theresa lived in a nice house in northeast Philadelphia. She was stable and had a husband and daughter.

Her answer was yes.

I remember the day clearly. I was out on the street with my mother, stumbling around, when I saw my aunt walking toward us. Words were exchanged. There were shouts. I felt my aunt's hands on my arms, being led into a waiting car. And then I was being driven away.

Without my mother.

I won't lie and say I wasn't sad. It's always frightening to be removed from your mother. But stronger than that feeling was my sense of relief, because I knew at least I was going somewhere safe.

I lived with my aunt Theresa, my uncle Giuseppe, and my cousin Victoria for about four months, during which my mother remained out on the street with Eddie, drinking and abusing pills. During this time, even while he was incarcerated, my father managed to support me financially with regular payments to Theresa.

This was a challenging time for me. Though I felt safe with my relatives, I still was afraid that Eddie and my mother would try to steal me from my aunt Theresa's house. In fact, I actually slept with my cousin Victoria to help alleviate this anxiety. Victoria was my godmother, actually, since she was nearly eighteen years old, and it was very nice of her to humor me.

Honestly, though, I sometimes felt like a burden to my relatives. They did show me love, and they never denigrated me, but I remember feeling that they were simply there to clean up my parents' mess. In other words, I never felt truly wanted by them. This was the first time that I can remember feeling judged by people for my parents' actions. So I would overcompensate and strive to be "perfect" and well-behaved, based on their standards, so as not to disappoint them further. The older I grew, the more my perfectionistic desire grew as well. I did not want to be perceived in the same manner in which my parents were: as complete "fuck-ups." This eventually translated into an effort to please others, so I learned how to be intuitive of others' ideals and perceptions.

And it all started in my aunt Theresa's home.

My Grandmother and The Return of My Father

Living in Theresa's home was a revelation. Things that other people took for granted seemed miraculous. A pot roast or plate of pasta on the table every night. Bedsheets and clothing washed and changed regularly. A dresser in which to put my clothes.

I had learned to take care of myself because my mother hadn't been doing it. At such a young age, it was a relief to have an outside force, like my aunt, take away that responsibility.

Still, though, I missed my father. To be honest, at that time, I didn't even know that he'd gone to prison. My family members had told me that he'd gone away to the "fat farm" to lose weight. It was a good story, and I believed it. (Ironically enough, he appeared to gain more weight while he was gone.)

But my father's need to protect me was strong. From prison, he asked my aunt Theresa to write a letter to the judge presiding over his case. He asked her to explain that my mother was unstable, that someone had to care for me, and then to request he be released from prison early. My aunt did so. She asked that the judge take my mother's situation into consideration and allow my father to complete his prison sentence under "the guidelines of community supervision," better known as parole.

It worked. The judge agreed to release my father from prison early.

Even though I was four years old, I remember my aunt taking me to court that day. I remember the adults towering over me; their dress shoes, the buzzing of fluorescent overhead lights. After the judge honored the request to release my father early, I remember my aunt handing me over to him. I ran toward his legs and he scooped me up into his arms.

If I wasn't exactly safe, this was the closest I would get.

Our living situation became awkward for a long time. Although my aunt had helped my father get out of prison, he would no longer allow me to see her. My father knew of my mother's slide into addiction and vagrancy. He also knew who my mother was with. He no longer wanted me exposed to the danger that my mother represented. And although I had seemed safe at Theresa's, he was afraid Theresa would allow my mother back into my life.

First, we went to my maternal grandmother, Mommom Rosie, hoping she would take us in. She was a full-blooded southern Italian-Calabrese, which is a nice way of saying that she was hard-headed, or as the Italians say, "capa tosta." My Mommom Rosie suffered from bipolar I disorder. Her mood fluctuations were severe. When she was manic, she partied with my mom, dad, and all of their friends. Other times she danced in the kitchen while cooking for strangers she'd met at Friends Psychiatric Hospital. (She was an exquisite authentic Italian cook.) But when her mood would fluctuate to depression, she would sleep twenty hours a day and remain in bed for days at a time. This was the kind of mother that my mom and her sisters grew up with.

Ultimately, she refused to allow my father and me to move in. Maybe she viewed my father as too much trouble, having once fallen into dealing methamphetamines for my father. But retrospectively, I believe Mommom turned my father and me away because she was so angry with my father for abandoning my mother when he would do jail time because of his illegal, crazy lifestyle. A little hypocritical, I know. In some way, by turning us away, I think she was trying to remain loyal to my mother, her daughter, while simultaneously sticking it to my father; I just happened to be collateral damage. I do think she felt bad about rejecting me because for the remainder of her life, and well into my adult life, she always had my back. She would help pay for my school tuition (Catholic elementary school and private Catholic girls' high school) and bailed my parents out of financial trouble more times than anyone could count. I was her favorite and she was mine, and everyone else in the family knew it. This caused some tension between me and my godmother, Victoria. But I had two dreadful parents, and she had two awesome parents (Aunt Theresa and Uncle Giuseppe), so give me a break!

Next, we went to Nana's (my father's mother) house in the Badlands. Nana accepted us right away. It makes sense: Her son was fresh out of prison, carting his young daughter with him because my mother was on drugs. From my adult perspective, Nana couldn't say no. We clearly needed help.

Once my mother learned of our whereabouts, she repeatedly tried to visit me. It was the same scenario every time. I remember her knocking on the door, exchanging sharp words with my father, then the sound of the door slamming. This went on for a few months.

Finally, my father relented.

When I saw my mother again, it wasn't pretty. She'd physically declined and had grown painfully thin. Her eyes carried that fifty-yard stare you see in people who're battling something enormous inside. She held me to her for a long time, clasped tight against her chest.

As for me, I remember staring out over my mother's shoulder, feeling scared, anxious, and worried that Eddie would torment us, which he did, until my dad and uncle beat him with a nightstick. But I was happy to know that she was safe too and that she and my dad were back together.

So much for our grand reunion.

I've felt that same anxious way about my mother many times since then. It's emotional moments like these that have always been the hardest for me to endure with my mother.

The reason is profound: My mother has made me feel so unsafe, during so many periods of my life, that I feel the tables have turned in our relationship. I have to protect her from herself. Her providing anything positive for me, even affection, is just not something I'm comfortable with receiving. I'm much more accustomed to the anxiety and instability she's projected onto me for years. It's hard to understand unless you've been in the situation.

What is unique about the way I see my own mother, since becoming a mother myself, is the way she interacts with my son, Gregory, and my daughter, Natalee. She is very loving, protective, and patient with them. Seeing her in this light has strengthened my relationship with her. I feel like, for my mom, her grandchildren are almost like a "do-over" for her and a way for her to make up for the way she parented or did not parent me because of her addiction and her mental health issues.

Today, from my standpoint, as a mental health professional, it's easier to understand what was going on inside of me. From childhood to adulthood, I've always felt I was mourning the loss of an idealized mother figure who I never had the fortune of knowing.

That is why my relationship with my Mommom Rosie was so important to me—I felt safe with her.

CHAPTER TWO

THE BADLANDS

Two-Room Efficiency

I t was a two-room efficiency. One main room, one bedroom, with a shared bathroom in the hallway. There was no kitchen, only a hot plate and a sink. And there were roaches everywhere.

After my mother moved back in with my father and me, this became our home for the next four years.

The building belonged to a slumlord. My dad tried to buy the building from him because he had a pipe dream to renovate it, but it never happened because back taxes were owed on the property, and the neighborhood was growing progressively worse. It was on the corner of Tulip Street and Lehigh Avenue. Nana lived directly below us, on the first floor, in the same two-room efficiency. The units were barely habitable by humans.

We were in the Badlands.

But it was a stable place to call home, and we didn't have to share it with anybody, or rely on anybody's goodwill. Curiously, this was a function of how my father's change in lifestyle from drug dealer to trying to make an honest living affected our lifestyle. We took a hit and endured a vastly lower standard of living.

During this period, my father cleaned up his act. He had wisely stopped dealing drugs, but then immediately ran into the wall faced by cons trying to walk the straight and narrow: He had a ninth-grade education, and nothing else. He also had no formal training or particular skills beyond being, shall we say, "entrepreneurial."

I remember him stewing about this for a while. There were tense meals. One day, he hit upon a solution.

"Maybe I should open a store," he said.

My mother looked at him. "Where you gonna open it? It costs money to lease."

The next day, he asked around, and he came steaming into the efficiency apartment with a glow around his head like we'd never seen.

"I found it," he said.

My father explained that the rooming house we were living in had a basement level that had once been a general store many years before. An external staircase that led down into it. The space wasn't free, but it was as close to free as an aspiring store owner could get. After talking it over with my mother, he decided to convert the old basement back into a convenience store.

He named the store Little Geri's, after me.

I was too young to understand how my parents were putting the business together, but I do remember that they designed it to be an old-fashioned convenience store. My father stocked the cheap shelving with inexpensive items like bread, milk, eggs, and other staples. To satisfy the sweet tooth of the neighborhood, he also sold candy, Italian ice, and hand-dipped ice cream. But the store's earnings were meager, no matter how many hours he put in behind the counter.

It was a poor neighborhood, and nothing was going to bring more money into the register.

I want to be clear on my feelings about the neighborhood. Despite its name, living in the Badlands wasn't really that bad. People had their troubles, and you did have to watch your step outside, but as a child, most of that flew over my head. I wasn't a target of the gangs or the drug dealers, and so I moved about unbothered.

But the Badlands is definitely bad for many adults. Located in north-central Philadelphia, the neighborhood earned its nickname from a novel, Third and Indiana, written by Steve Lopez, who was a columnist for The Philadelphia Inquirer. Physically, it's not much to look at—rows of redbrick houses punctuated by empty factories, which had been abandoned when the local industries fled the city to developing countries such as Mexico and India.

Mostly the neighborhood was infamous for its open-air drug markets. I learned to identify those areas and avoid them. The corner of 3rd Street and Indiana was one of the most drug-infested intersections in the nation.

But it did present its challenges, mostly from the other children in the neighborhood. I was constantly forced to defend myself against boys and girls alike, many of whom ran feral and free. They saw some-thing in me they didn't like, maybe a sense of self-worth, maybe my innate desire to better myself. The bucket of crabs metaphor—the idea that any crab trying to escape the bucket is grabbed and pulled back by the others—definitely applied to my life.

I remember one instance when the Jones family lived across the street from us. There were eight or nine children living in the home. The youngest girl, Crystal, two years older than I, would constantly pick on me. She would shove me and intimidate me. I told my parents about it, and that's when my father taught me how to "hold my hands" and defend myself. Mind you; I was probably five or six years old. After giving me a boxing lesson and pep talk on sticking up for myself, Dad insisted that Crystal envied me because of my looks.

Whatever the case may have been, Crystal, per usual, started with me one day. I was strolling down the street, my purse full of "girly things" like my mom's old lipsticks, when Crystal intentionally blocked the sidewalk and shoved me.

I could hear my father yelling from the doorway of the store, "Don't take any shit from her Ger, crack her."

With that, I took my purse off my shoulder and swung it, whacking Crystal in the face. She was stunned, but rather than give her a chance to recover, I used the move my dad showed me: I grabbed her long hair, yanked her head down, and punched her face two or three times. Crystal ran away, and I ran back into the store, where I received an "Atta girl" and a high five from my dad. True to bully form, Crystal stopped bullying me.

My father continued to teach me how to fight, telling me, "not to take shit from anyone." I remember my father pulling me out into the street one evening, crouching down behind me, showing me how to knock away an unwanted arm, how to punch from the body, how to kick a man in the testicles. Then he made me demonstrate on him, falling over on the concrete in mock pain.

Throughout my life, my father often took the time to discuss subjects with me that I doubt other parents would broach, spliced with bits of examples from his own, um, illuminating life. He told me about avoiding drug addiction, urging me not to end up "with a monster inside you" (his term for drug addiction), not to get on the wrong side of the law, "like your mother and me."

So that was my daily life at this time. Living near open-air drug markets while being told to stay the hell away from all drugs. Life need not make sense, I guess.

Plus, as if my childhood wasn't unstable enough, I also suffered from frequent fainting spells. Starting from not even two years old, I would faint everywhere—in school, at church, at family functions, and especially when I was sick. These fainting spells went un- or misdiagnosed for many years. I went to a variety of specialists, some of whom thought I suffered from epilepsy, while others tested me for leukemia. Ultimately, a cardiologist diagnosed me at age twelve with vasovagal syncope. It's an otherwise benign condition that occurs when an environmental trigger, the sight of blood, perhaps, causes your heart rate and blood pressure to drop suddenly. It still affects me from time to time, and I've learned to avoid the things that trigger it, such as standing for a long period of time in the heat, the sight of blood, lack of sleep, or high levels of stress.

We made some positive strides at one point. We started talking to my mother's family again—Mommom, Aunt Theresa, Uncle Giuseppe, and my cousin Victoria. My mother worked consistently as a hairdresser during this period, too.

But there was no escaping the drama. Eddie came nosing around our house, usually fortified by Irish courage. He'd bang on the door and loudly challenge my father to a fight. Other times, Eddie would often show up at the apartment on a ten-speed bike while trying to get my mother's attention. Every time my father would run outside to go after him, Eddie would speed off. (A friend of my father's, lovingly referred to as Psycho John, would from time to time chase Eddie down and "beat his ass.")

The battles continued, and expanded in scope. Mom told Dad that it was Aunt Marge who had "narced" on him, sending him to jail. When somehow Marge learned this, she went berserk. I know Marge should have been the last one in this scenario to be upset, but she had little logic and less sense. Marge reacted in typical Kenzo (Kensington) fashion.

I remember my mother's hands gripping me tightly as aunt Marge tore up the steps and began beating my mother in the face as she held me on her hip. I was terrified as the assault went on for what felt like, in memory's rearview mirror, hours. Then, after Marge left, my mother's face was so swollen that she was nearly unrecognizable. She stumbled downstairs to my grandmother's unit, pleading for help. I remember all three of us taking a cab to the emergency room, where my mother was quickly rushed into a room and treated for her injuries. It took over a week for the swelling to subside, and her face was horribly decorated with bruises for nearly a month.

After that, my father didn't speak to Cholly or Marge for three years. It was like they didn't exist. And every time I think of the Badlands, I think of that assault, especially because it didn't come from a stranger but from family.

***

Little Geri's convenience store wasn't doing well. It was a failure to launch, though you could say that nobody had filled the rocket's fuel tanks. After all, nobody in the neighborhood had any money, and even if they had, how much dough could you really make slinging milk, eggs, and candy? My father had entered the business so positive and hopeful, but as time went on, the failure took its toll. His temper grew shorter. But he rarely drank when we lived on Tulip Street. He also stopped doing and dealing meth at this time, which was a welcome change.

"I gotta find another job," he said one night.

My mother was standing in the bathroom in her yellow robe, hair up, looking at herself in the mirror. She was plucking her eyebrows. I remember that she was still attractive at that time, even after she'd abused so many substances.

"What do you want to do?" she said.

"I don't know, but we gotta get out of this neighborhood like you have been pushing us to do," he said.

"All right," my mom said.

He sat on the edge of the chair, his arms on his knees, his head hanging down.

My mother then sat and talked with my dad for hours about legal ways to make money and get out of the neighborhood.

Soon after that, he partnered with an old childhood friend, and together they began doing concrete and brick point work. The name of the company was U.S. Brick Pointing. My father, in true Jerry Utter fashion, had very nice business cards designed with the company logo, which had little stars for the periods in between U.S. He had them embossed in a maroon color so that he could go out, market the business, and get customers.

Construction was how so many men from the neighborhood found themselves, and it saved my father and me. With some effort, his new masonry business did well enough that my father closed downed the short-lived convenience store. Soon after that, he'd saved enough money for us to move to Northeast Philadelphia.

We left the Badlands.

I remember little of that day, but I do remember hearing the door to the two-bedroom efficiency close for the final time behind me. As we descended the stairs for the last time to the street outside, I remember feeling happy.

My life was just beginning, but I was already looking forward to a better way of life.

It would be a long time before I got there.

Lunch with Mom

It was lunchtime at my new Catholic elementary school. I'd started going there a few weeks earlier and found myself with a whole new group of friends. Many of them came from stable, healthy families, which was not in the cards for anybody in the old neighborhood. There were even a couple of nuns who were still teaching at the school, and I found myself toeing a strict dress code, the usual white blouse and plaid jumper.

Every day, we ate lunch on top of our desks. It was strange, and unsanitary, if you ask me – the same desk we did our classwork on all day, we ate our lunch on. We had to bring a small kitchen towel to place on top of our desks as not to get them dirty and stained with food. If someone forgot their towel, they would receive a demerit.

You gotta love Catholic school.

On this day, my mother was bringing lunch for me. I couldn't bear to face her, especially here. Her behavior had been unpredictable when we had lived on the streets, and I was still jumpy at the sight of her. As she entered the classroom, I nearly panicked, worried that mom would say or do something crazy and embarrass me in front of the class.

Admittedly, she had usually been able to pull it off in front of school staff and students. But my stomach would be in knots the remainder of the day because I knew what awaited me at home. I knew it would be an all-out war when my dad came home from work and could end with my father putting his hands on my mom. I dreaded those days.

I was lucky on this day. She was clear-eyed and coherent, and we exchanged pleasantries as I ate my lunch.

That was it.

Proving again that when she was sober, our interactions were warm. Some days, she would surprise me by bringing me Burger King when she was a lunch monitor. And, her behavior was like that of a hawk, watching me at a safe distance, but ensuring I was okay. Because I fainted a lot in school, my mother would volunteer so that she could check on me. She was also like my bodyguard. If anyone messed with me during recess, she would "put them on the wall," which was a sort of time-out where you had to stand and face a brick wall. Most kids were smart enough not to mess with her.

Yes, greater Northeast Philadelphia was a different world, and it overall changed my life for the better.

To my surprise, it impacted my parents' relationship most of all. My father continued to work in the contracting business, and my mother continued to work as a hairdresser. For the most part, things approached normal, or at least as "normal" as they could be for us. To steal a line from the film Raising Arizona, it wasn't Ozzie and Harriet, and never would be. But we improved.

In fact, my mother suddenly became very obedient to my father, displaying the old-school Italian values of waiting on your husband hand and foot. Aside from when he was in jail, she was always very obedient and loyal to my father, despite him cheating on her.

I can't forget seeing the change. My mother in the kitchen, pulling dinner out of the oven while my father and I sat at the dinner table, me in my favorite t-shirt and pants, him in a tee and his post-work track pants.

"You want something to drink?" she asked him.

"Milk."

He never had to get up to pour himself that glass of milk. My mother would do it for him. She was happy to serve him. It was a form of gratitude for the changes that had occurred in their shared lives.

Although my mother was 100% Italian, my father hated most Italian food. So, she learned how to cook medigan (non-Italian) food from my Nana. Most nights, she would make meals like steak and mashed potatoes and green beans, pork chops and mashed potatoes with gravy and peas, or meatloaf with mashed potatoes and green beans. My father was a very picky eater, but my mom did manage to fatten him up. With every meal he would drink a tall glass of milk and six buttered pieces of bread! I remember him placing mashed potatoes on a single piece of buttered bread and folding it into a mashed potato sandwich of sorts. For her and me, she would often make a salad or a different side other than homemade mashed potatoes. As delicious as they were, we didn't like to eat mashed potatoes every single night like my dad! Nonetheless, she peeled, boiled, and hand-mashed potatoes for my father at least five nights a week.

It was true that my dad had changed for the better. Instead of vanishing from the house for days on end while dealing and abusing meth, my father was now working a respectable construction job. He actually remained faithful in the marriage now. And he was packing on the pounds from my mother's new calorie-laden, home-cooked meals, but nobody held that against him.

There was one curious thing, though, that hinted at the fact that their issues were not dead, but merely in deep hibernation. It was this: my parents slept in their bedroom, but at night, my father unrolled a cot, and my mother slept on a makeshift mattress next to him. This lasted way too long to be normal, and I don't know if it's ever been really explained, but I think my mother's infidelity with Eddie turned my father off. I believe they were together for me, and in some weird way, the arrangement worked for both of them. He kept my mother stable and in-line and she did the same for him.

Still they were happy. I was happy. The world was pretty good.

But it wouldn't last.

The Monster Returns

During this time, my mother began to engage in a pattern of binge drinking.

She would abstain from booze for a period of time, usually weeks, sometimes even months. She appeared normal; behaved as normally as possible. She acted lovingly towards both me and my father. This was Mrs. Jekyll.

Then the metamorphosis would begin. Some inner demon would drive my mother to begin drinking and she wouldn't stop, not for days. It was more than a pleasant indulgence. She would get plastered, snookered, wasted, lit, epically shit-faced, without any seeming governor on her behavior. I could smell the booze seeping out of her pores.

When I would come home from school and see that she had been hitting the bottle, I would ask, "Mom, have you been drinking?"

To which she would softly reply, "No, Geri."

With that, I had to validate my suspicions and reassure myself that I wasn't going crazy, so I searched the house. But the search wasn't much of a challenge as my mom was terrible at covering her tracks; hiding pint bottles of Canadian Windsor under piles of clothes, under the bathroom sink, and under couch cushions.

On one particular occasion, I remember her spraying perfume (yes, expensive perfume) on her tongue because she thought it would rid her of the smell of alcohol.

Her benders would typically last a day or two, but the damage and upheaval it created in the home took weeks to recover from.

Many times, I anxiously awaited my dad's arrival home from work. I would beg my mom not to argue with him. The booze gave her liquid courage and with that a voice, an opinion, in the marriage.

That's when Mrs. Hyde would arrive.

The taunting that came out of my mother's mouth during those binges was astounding. She transformed into an aggressive, angry, verbally-abusive drunk. She picked fights with my father, and if he didn't give her one, she kept hammering at him until he did. It was as though the alcohol allowed her to express all of the hurt and resentment that had built up against my father over the years. Quite frankly, I feel as though it was the only time that my mother actually seemed to have a voice in the marriage.

Unfortunately, these moments never failed to end in a vicious clash between my parents. They fought like two cats in a bag. My mother's vociferous mouth would enrage my father, and then he would physically beat her. Not a small man, he stood six feet, three inches, and at that time weighed around three hundred pounds.

In short, their conflict followed a typical pattern: verbal abuse from her, then physical abuse from him.

I don't want to sugarcoat this. It was horrific. There were many times when I watched my mother laying on the family couch, flat on her back, drunk, taunting my father with name-calling, mockery, complaints. My father sat nearby in his beloved overstuffed chair, trying to either defuse her or ignore her, but neither worked. A fuse shorted in his brain, he always snapped. When that happened, my father usually stood up, walked over to the couch, and punched my mother right in her face as she lay there.

I told you that it was horrific.

Remember that I am an only child. When I witnessed those fights, I was beyond scared—I felt devastated, as though the world were ending. Their effect on me has been extremely powerful, and it has definitely affected multiple areas of my life as an adult.

Sometimes I even tried to get between them, to break up those battles, since nobody else was there to do it. I remember running toward my father and trying to grab his arm and pull him off of my mother, but it was as if I were a flea and he was a gorilla. He didn't even acknowledge my feeble attempt.

The days following these abusive events were very, very sad. My mother's eyes would be so black and blue and swollen shut that on one occasion, when I saw her, I literally fainted. My father, usually sociable and talkative, was solemn, quiet, and regretful. Dinners were eaten in resounding silence, three pairs of eyes afraid to meet.

He always apologized to my mother for putting his hands on her, and my mother always forgave him. Then peace returned to the house. For a while. Sadly, I knew that I had only a month or so before the next battle would ensue. But at least it gave me some relief.

It was a dysfunctional cycle, and I was dragged into it.

You can imagine how difficult this was for an eight-year-old. My cries, screams, and efforts to physically prevent them from fighting never seemed to work. But I learned that calling the cops did. My fingers grew very adept, dancing across that old telephone dial pad. I can still recite the phone number of the police station to this day.

But when the police arrived, my mother always refused to press charges. This meant that my father was never arrested for putting his hands on her, not once in the years that he beat her. More often than not, I would see him cry afterward, holding his head in his hands upon realizing the effect that his violent outburst had had on both my mother and myself.

This cycle continued for four years, until my parents separated in 1993. It left a permanent wound on my brain and my heart.

New Arrivals

The more I listened to Mommom, the less sense she was making.

I remembered the day well. Her mouth was forming words, but only about half of them were understandable.

"Dearie pie," she said, "would you gustisloothforth a yuttey because I've got the costrulimersher?"

"What?" I said.

"It's the guwursherslee on the right."

She was pointing at something, but damned if I knew what.

My mother and I had just arrived in her apartment. Mommom Rosie was a very active, and young-looking old lady. She was shampooing heads with my mother at the hair salon where she worked well into her late 60s. But she had clearly just suffered another stroke.

"We're here to take you over to our place," my mother said, standing near the doorway with arms crossed.

Mommom looked confused. "Why is that?"

"You can't live on your own anymore."

It took a bit more cajoling, but the truth was that Mommom didn't have the strength to resist anybody or anything. She'd already suffered multiple ministrokes.

We moved her into our apartment the next day.

Mommom always looked out for me and cared for me deeply. Like my mother, she suffered from depression, but she always seemed to hold a soft spot for me. The closeness of our relationship was often a source of tension with my older cousin, Victoria; however, as a child, I didn't recognize how profoundly my cousin was affected by it.

My mother and my grandmother's relationship was also very close, and even though my father was not Italian, she had a soft spot for him, too. She still referred to him and his preferred meals as medigan, though! Despite the fact that we lived in a small apartment, she found it comfortable to be living with us, particularly my parents.

When I asked my mom about Mommom Rosie and their relationship, she stated, "she was never really there for me. When she was depressed, she would stay in bed for weeks, and my aunt Vicki and neighbor Vera took care of us because by that time, my dad had already died. She never really showed me any affection. But everyone loved my mom; she would take people in, like my best friend Nancy (at age 15), who didn't have a good home life. She was the life of the party and fed everyone.".

This description very much reminds me of my own relationship with my mother. This is an interesting generational pattern- my grandmother's mental health issues, drinking and dependence to pain meds prevented her from parenting my mother well (i.e. my mother feeling loved) and my mother's addiction and mental health issues prevented her from parenting me well. Oddly enough, both my grandmother (with me) and my mother (with my kids) have developed a loving and affectionate bond with their grandchildren.

Eventually, however, the side effects of my grandmother's strokes exacerbated her depression. While staying with us, she was in and out of psychiatric hospitals for over a year and even received Electro-Convulsive Therapy or ECT. At the time, it was difficult for me to see my grandmother so sick because we spent a lot of time together.

A year later, Mommom moved in with my aunt Theresa. It was a short period of time before Theresa placed her in a nursing home. My parents worked as hard as they could to oppose this, to keep my grandmother out of the nursing home, but the strain of taking care of her, compounded by their marital problems, proved too formidable. Ultimately, her failing health and my aunt's desire outweighed my parents' will to keep her with us.

Around that time, my aunt Marge died of stomach cancer. Her daughters, my cousins Ronni and Amber, moved in with us. It was unusual, but my father decided to put them into our two-bedroom apartment because their dad, my uncle Cholly, was an alcoholic and drug user who verbally and physically abused them. (In their presence, Uncle Cholly often referred to his daughters as "little whores" and "fat pigs." They were 10 and 13 years old at the time. This abuse only worsened after Marge's death.)

Ronni was a year older than me. She had low self-esteem because she was overweight, and her father never let her forget it. Amber's problems were more severe, in particular, a history of promiscuity and various behavioral and drug-related issues; in fact, my father picked Amber up from Belmont Psychiatric Hospital when we took her in.

My cousins referred to me as the "snobby princess" – quite a startling accusation, considering how I had grown up. But I went to Catholic school, I lived in a better part of the city, and my parents were doing their best to provide for me. Everything is relative; to them, I was living in a castle made of cotton candy.

Things didn't go very well. Amber was drinking booze and smoking weed in the house. Add to that the number of men we caught her with, in various stages of undress, and it wasn't long before my parents had had enough. Particularly my mother, with whom Amber argued incessantly.

In the end, my parents kicked Amber out of our home after only six months. Ronni stayed with us a few more years, until we later got evicted from the apartment on Garvey Drive.

CHAPTER THREE

THINGS GET BAD

Utter Nonsense

The construction business had slowed at this time, and my father was out of work. He continued singing in the Destinations, but they booked gigs only occasionally. Fortunately, my grandmother helped out our family, but it wasn't enough to cover every expense.

That's when Uncle Cholly stepped in to save the day. Yes, the alcoholic, abusive drug addict who mocked his own daughters did something uncharacteristically nice, though, of course, something that could lead to more trouble.

He got my father a job tending bar.

With him.

The bar was called Dee-Dee's, and it was located at the corner of D and Somerset streets in Kensington. This was deep in the heart of the Badlands, the same place we'd just escaped from a few years earlier. With no other choice, my father accepted his new job slinging cocktails every night from 4 pm until 2 am.

I don't imagine my father was very happy, but the opportunity came just in time, because soon after that Uncle Cholly was stabbed.

Turns out, Cholly had been running around with his best friend's wife. When Cholly's best friend Harry learned of the affair, he took his revenge by repeatedly stabbing Cholly in the torso.

Uncle Cholly's injury was so serious that it severely damaged his liver, spleen, intestines, and the lining of his stomach. He was lucky to have lived. Despite this, he continued his alcoholic ways, pouring liquor down his throat like dishwater down a kitchen drain.

It was around that time when my father began to talk to my mother about buying the bar, which he cleverly intended to rename "Utter Nonsense." She supported the idea, but there was no getting around the fact that they just did not have the finances to do so. Furthermore, my father, a convicted felon with a rap sheet 20 pages long, doubted he would be approved by the Liquor Control Board (LCB) for a liquor license as they ran routine background checks on individuals who applied for a license.

This is why, he explained, he would need my mother to put the liquor license in her name. This would forever be a source of conflict.

Just Say No

While my dad was making plans to buy the bar, I was starting to feel my first outside pressure to drink. I was in the eighth grade, and my friends began drinking and experimenting with drugs. I heard their stories of the keg parties on the weekends. I remember the girl who sneaked a joint into the bathroom at lunchtime. And the other guy who huffed paint thinner. But I never joined them.

I've reflected a lot about why I never took drugs or alcohol. A lot of this had to do with the way my father talked to me as a child. The conversations ran like this:

"Geri-Lynn," he would say, "I dropped outta school and it was the biggest mistake I ever made."

"I know," I would say.

"And then I found drugs, and that was my other major mistake."

I would nod my head. He wasn't necessarily a religious man, but I knew my dad would continue to describe addiction in religious terms.

"See, Geri," he would say, "it's like being possessed by the devil. It really is. At first, you think they're cool, but then you realize that you've gotten possessed by some kind of demon, and he causes you to become a person you don't wanna be."

We would have most conversations in the living room. He sat in his tan corduroy chair, leaning forward, smoking a cigarette (he smoked four packs of Kool's a day), and I sat on the floor across from him on the ottoman that matched his chair. I would listen quietly and not interrupt. The subject was important to him. I also enjoyed listening to him. He had a way about him, where you never felt lectured when he was giving you advice. And even then, I realized that he knew what the hell he was talking about.

"I was stealing, manipulating, lying. Those drugs turned me into somebody I didn't know. Heroin put me in goddamn prison. And speed, don't even get me started on that."

Sometimes I would keep it rolling by asking little questions. "What's that like?"

My dad would grow animated; his eyes widening as he recalled something from his past. "Speed rots your body from the inside out. I mean, I thought heroin was bad, but going from heroin to speed was like going from the frying pan into the fire. It is like the devil has you by the short hairs."

"Oh."

Then he would look at me. "I love you, kid, that's why I'm telling you this. Don't make my mistakes."

"I won't," I would say.

"I believe in you. I believe in you like you wouldn't even believe, Gerawin (his form of pet name for me). You can do anything you put your mind to. Anything at all."

We must've had this same conversation fifty times. After hearing it so often, I came to believe it. I still remember his words every time I am faced with a challenge and start to doubt myself. My dad always had faith in me, even when I didn't have faith in myself. And his words, even during the years when I wasn't speaking with him, resonated with me, remaining there during the most challenging of times.

He influenced the way I perceive myself.

For the better.

I am grateful to my dad for this, regardless of how highly dysfunctional he was in other aspects of his life.

***

But there was another reason for my disinterest in drugs or alcohol.

It was around this time that I walked into the community center near our apartment at two o'clock on a Saturday afternoon. I went down the hall, feeling a pit opening up in my stomach.

The room was large and lit by overhead fluorescent lights. About fifteen folding chairs waited on the floor. Stacks of Styrofoam cups and a pitcher of lemonade had been set up on a folding table at the side of the room. Someone met me near the door and greeted me nicely. I signed in with my name.

It was my first Al-Anon meeting. Alateen, to be precise.

I sat down quietly and waited for the meeting to begin. One by one, people began trickling into the meeting room. I saw middle school students and high school students. Mostly I was relieved to see other kids my own age there. It was particularly comforting to know that there were other kids my own age who'd been affected by alcoholism, who had parents who suffered with this disease.

The meeting started with a group greeting. Then, as the attendees began to share their experiences, I found myself mesmerized by their stories. Some had been beaten. Some had been mocked and insulted. And worse. And all by someone in their life addicted to drugs or alcohol.

One girl's story stuck with me. Marjorie. She was a couple years older than I and was a star student at her high school. Every night she came home, made dinner for herself, then went up to her room to do her homework. Her mother would arrive home at about 9 pm, already half in the bag, and proceed to throw herself on the sofa and begin drinking. When Marjorie was finished with her homework, at about eleven pm, she'd head downstairs, snap off the television, collect the empty liquor or beer bottles, and put them in the recycling. Then she would pick up her mother and physically carry her, like a Sherpa climbing a mountain, to her bedroom.

Marjorie was only fifteen years old. Though my experience wasn't exactly the same as hers, I recognized something.

She was me; I was her.

As the meeting went on, I soon discovered something else: that although I related very well to others like Marjorie, the feelings they evoked in me made me uncomfortable. I had never been forced to address my own issues stemming from my parents' disease, and I didn't like it. This was made crystal clear as I was listening to her, and at that moment, I began to cry. For the first time, I was intensely vulnerable. I did not like feeling that way, and I definitely did not want to be pitied by anybody. I left the community center that day feeling like someone had just put me in an emotional blender and flicked it on high.

In retrospect, I realize now that feeling vulnerable and crying are useful emotions for children and teens in my and Marjorie's situation. This meeting helped my interior wall begin to crumble and, although it left me feeling very raw, it was intensely therapeutic and set me on my long path to healing.

The Departure of My Father ...Again

Around this time, my mother wanted to prove that my father was fooling around on her. Apparently, she'd heard rumors from the neighbors, and she wanted proof. This wasn't so much for herself, but for me and my cousin Ronni. You see, we both idealized my father, despite his flaws, and didn't want to believe that he could be having an affair. I think my mother felt as though we all thought she was crazy to think anything was going on, and to be honest, it felt better believing that she was crazy then to accept the sad reality that my father was cheating on her. Accepting that my father had been cheating on my mother equated to losing all sense of stability we had. It was at this point that the "D" word (divorce) was being thrown around a lot, and it scared us. I didn't want my life to revert back to what it was like when my mother was with Eddie. I felt anxious and unsafe at that time. I didn't want those feelings to return.

My mother's plan involved Ronni and me. My dad had a singing gig at a bar, and my mother knew that the "other woman" would be there because Dad had insisted my mother was not allowed to come to the bar to hear him sing this time. (Keep in mind my mother never missed one of my father's shows; she was his number one fan.) So Mom decided to send Ronni and me into the bar as undercover operatives.

At my mother's insistence, Ronni and I took turns doing each other's make-up. I sat on the toilet while Ronni made up my face – mascara, eyeliner, lipstick, you name it. Then my mother handed me a fistful of tissue paper.

"What's this for?"

"Stuff it in your bra," my mother said. "It'll make you look older."

After we were all dolled up and able to pass as two young women of legal drinking age, we drove to the bar and skulked inside, where we spotted my father kissing a very close family friend, Diane. After seeing the "proof" of my father's infidelity with our own eyes, my mother began cursing, crying, and yelling at the pair. All three of us were tossed out of the bar and my father didn't even attempt to follow us out. It was as if we didn't exist.

Once we collected ourselves and did our best to calm my mother down, she proceeded to drop us off at the corner of Somerset and Auburn Street in the Badlands. It was 1:30 in the morning, and we were two young girls dressed up with make-up on our faces and tissue paper in our bras.

"Where are you going?"

"To meet Eddie."

Of course, she meant Eddie O'Brien. The same Eddie with whom she had had a relationship while my father was incarcerated. The same Eddie that I had wandered the streets with for all those months when I was four years old. The same Eddie who used to show up on our doorstep, drunk, challenging my father to a fistfight that he always lost.

I couldn't believe my ears. The family dysfunction had returned, like the proverbial monster rising out of the lake after he was supposed to be drowned.

Because my mother dropped us off in the old neighborhood, we were able to knock on a neighbor's door and ask to use the phone. Keep in mind, this was before cell phones and mobile devices were a thing, especially in this part of town. We called the bar and asked to speak with my father. We told him where we were and explained that we had no way of getting back home.

What felt like hours later, my father pulled up in his pickup truck, and I headed out to meet him. He handed me a bag.

"Take a cab home," he said, handing me a few dollars.

"But why are you—"

He cut me off. "Don't ask questions, just go, right now. Don't stand here on the street corner, Geri. Get home!"

"But Mom dropped me off here."

He looked at me. "Yeah, she's lost her mind. Hey, one more thing. Don't open that bag until you get home. You hear me?"

"Yes."

My father pointed at me.

"Get out of here. I'll be home in the morning. I'll see you in the morning."

Then he raced off. Ronni and I found a cab and rode home, feeling confused by the drama that was unfolding.

Safe and sound inside our house, I locked the door behind me, hid the bag in my underwear drawer, and then sat down next to it. Part of me didn't want to know what my dad was involved in.

But I couldn't resist the temptation.

With Ronni standing over my shoulder, I slowly unzipped the bag. Inside I saw several small bricks of twenty-dollar bills, neatly rubber-banded together for easy transport.

I did a quick count. It was over ten thousand dollars.

Later, I learned that my father had reached out to old acquaintances from the Irish mob to borrow money for the down payment to buy the bar.

And the only person he trusted to carry the money was me.

Over the weeks and months that followed, my parents fought constantly. They fought about alcohol, about drugs, about money, about Eddie, about Diane, about other men, about other women, about Ronni, and about me. The masks were off.

Finally, my mother kicked my father out of the house. He moved in with Diane down in the Badlands. I remember having mixed feelings seeing him leave—the person who'd loved me the most was leaving me, but at the same time, he'd invited a lot of chaos into my life.

No sooner was he gone than Eddie moved into our house. Straight into my mother's bedroom. Literally taking the place of my father.

His presence made my skin crawl.

All of those old emotions that I had felt as a young child came rushing back like a tidal wave. I had been fearful of Eddie due to his aggressive and unpredictable nature. When Eddie and Mother got back together, he had actually been clean and sober for three years. But my mother was still drinking. And, when you think about addiction and recovery, a large part of sustaining abstinence is related to the places and faces users associate with. My mother's instability and drinking triggered Eddie to relapse, despite his efforts to maintain his sobriety while encouraging my mother to do the same.

The two of them together, again, were locked in a toxic embrace of addictive dysfunction. At least my mother and father had maintained a semblance of normality, however slim. But Eddie was different. This was a lethally bad relationship.

In me, it evoked all those feelings of being unsafe, unprotected, and vulnerable to whatever consequences came about.

Once again, I was collateral damage.

A New Baby

By the end of my freshman year of high school at Nazareth Academy, a private Catholic college preparatory school for girls, my mother had become a heroin addict. Eddie worked as a roofer and furniture deliveryman.

No sooner had he moved in, than he began pestering my mother to get pregnant. I think he'd been deeply jealous of my father and wanted to displace him by all available means; impregnating my mother seemed a good way to do that.

My mother was 43 years old at the time, so it wasn't an easy matter. And she was not at all interested in being a mother again. But she wanted to do anything she could to keep Eddie around. Him being ten years younger than she seemed to make my mother feel youthful.

She managed to get pregnant.

But the pregnancy wasn't simple. My mother had to be closely monitored because of her age. She was also depressed throughout the pregnancy because she regretted the pregnancy immensely. My mother began taking the pain medication Percocet under the guise of treating tooth pain. I believe a large part of it was self-medication of the emotional pain as she had never dealt with my father's infidelity and the subsequent divorce.

She soon became addicted to Percocet and began purchasing them off the street. She was taking handfuls of the pills daily, even while pregnant with my sister. This was obviously stunningly wrong. My mother has since claimed that she started abusing pain medication prior to her pregnancy, but that is irrelevant. To get hooked on prescription pills with a second human growing in utero is abhorrently irresponsible. My mother's new drug use caused Eddie to join in her misery. Soon they were both using Percocet.

Then, five weeks before her due date, my mother gave birth to a new daughter. That's how, at age 14, I found myself with a newborn little half-sister.

I remember when my mom found out she was having a girl. On top of being depressed, she seemed even more depressed because she told me that she has always wanted a boy, even hoped that I would be a boy. (Gee, thanks, mom.) My mom gave me permission to name the new baby and one day before the baby was born, my mother was lying on her bed. I went into the room and talked with her. She confided in me that she had made a mistake getting pregnant and that she was afraid. I tried to make her feel better by telling her that I had already come up with a name for the baby girl, Dominique! I picked Dominique because I liked the name and because it was my confirmation name. She gave me a slight smile.

The Arrival of Jimmy-Joe

In high school, my cousin Ronni started delivering furniture with Eddie part-time. She began to miss a lot of school when she was a sophomore at a public high school, and I was a freshman at a parochial school.

My mother began to allow my friends to drink and party at my house, and often crash there. I, however, refused to drink, do drugs or sleep around, to the point that my friends called me "Sister Geri." Ironically, this young nun's mother was more than happy to allow her house to gain a reputation as a "party house" for everyone in my neighborhood. At best, it was a terribly misguided effort to monitor me and my behavior.

To be honest, I felt like I was the one monitoring her. And, after a time, it felt like I was monitoring the so-called friends that I was hanging out with at the time. They were part of the cool, troublemaking crowd. My father's words were still ringing in my ears, and I could see where such troublemakers eventually ended up.

At the end of the year, my mother allowed me to go to a New Year's Eve party. This was a rare night out for me. There I discovered a lot of older guys, mostly in their early twenties, many of them older brothers of my friends.

It was a rough party. I watched as a fight broke out, and a handsome guy pulled out an assault rifle and threatened to kill someone if he didn't clear out. We were all scared to death. The threatened person was escorted out. It seemed that the handsome guy carried some weight in the neighborhood.

Later that night, after things had calmed down, the handsome guy came up to me.

"Hey, you're that Geri-Lynn girl, yeah?"

"Yeah. Who're you?"

Truth be told, I knew who he was, everyone knew who he was. Justin, his very handsome younger brother, formally introduced us. You see, Justin had been staying with me because both Jimmy-Joe and Justin and Jimmy-Joe's mother, Terri, were doing state time on drug related charges.

"I'm Jimmy-Joe," he said.

"Nice to meet you."

He stood there, waiting to be recognized, narrowing his eyes at me. "So I'm Justin's brother, yeah?"

Justin said, "This is the girl with the mom, the cool one. You need anything, Geri-Lynn's mom has you covered."

It didn't surprise me that word had gotten out about my bizarre home life. I realized that people knew that my mother would often let my friends — or anyone with a sob story — move in with us. Young people like to gossip, and when someone's family is permissive, they gossip even more.

Several days later, my doorbell rang at around 11 o'clock at night. When I opened it, Jimmy-Joe was there, breathless, looking as though he were being chased by the cops. I immediately let him in and shut the door behind him.

"What's the matter?" I said.

"Nothing," he replied.

"You look scared, like someone is after you."

"They are," he said, "but they won't catch me."

Jimmy-Joe flopped down on the couch, let out a huge sigh, and tipped his head backwards, and closed his eyes.

I stood near the door, not knowing what to do.

Then he lifted his head and looked up at me.

"I'm hungry."

"We don't have anything to eat."

"Nothing?"

I shook my head. "My mom said she was gonna pick up some groceries but... she hasn't followed through."

A look of frustration passed across Jimmy-Joe's face. Then he looked like he'd just been struck by a brilliant thought.

"Hey, you wanna go get some food?"

My stomach had been growling. As my mother's consumption of Percocet had been increasing, her parenting skills had been decreasing, if possible. I went hungry a lot during this time.

"I guess so," I said.

"There's a 7-11 on the corner, yeah?"

I nodded. He was off the couch in a flash, and before I knew it, he'd pulled me down the staircase and out into the street.

"I thought you said someone was chasing you," I said.

He shrugged.

At the 7-11, Jimmy-Joe bought us a couple of hot dogs and some sodas. He also bought some staple groceries for our house because he knew we didn't have anything. We ate the hot dogs standing outside. His eyes were darting around nervously.

Nearby, parked behind the store, was a bread delivery truck.

"You still hungry, yeah?"

"Yeah," I said.

Without another word, he loped across the asphalt, picked the lock on the truck, rolled up the back, and leaped in. A few seconds later, he came out with an armful of bread.

He cocked his head to the side. "Let's go."

I followed him back home.

As we went back up the staircase to my apartment, Jimmy-Joe said, "Geri-Lynn, do you think I could spend the night? Just for one night."

I chose my words carefully. "I don't have a problem with it. You'll just have to ask my mom."

An hour later, my mother came home. When she walked in, Jimmy-Joe was sprawled out on our couch, watching television. He sat up, and politely asked my mom if he could stay. I was at the kitchen table, trying to concentrate on my algebra homework instead of on his crystal blue eyes.

"Who's this?" my mother said.

He said, "Jimmy-Joe, Justin's older brother. I met Geri at that New Year's party that you let her go to." He paused. "We're not together or nothing. It's just... you know, I needed a place to crash for a night. That's all right with you?"

I don't know why, but the conversation was mortifying. I wanted to hide myself away in a dark corner and never be found.

My mother looked the visitor up and down. "That's alright, stay as long as you need."

"Thank you, Mrs. Utter."

She walked into the kitchen. ""You can call me Jeanne. Jesus Christ, who bought all the bread?"

Jimmy-Joe stayed with us for almost four months.

***

Even though Jimmy-Joe engaged in criminal behavior, like threatening to kill someone with an M-16 assault rifle, I felt oddly safe in his presence. He provided a sense of security for me that my parents did not. My dad had left me to sleep with Diane, and my mom was attempting to "get her groove back" with Eddie. Selfish and consumed with their own lives, their concern for me had fallen by the wayside. With barely any food in the house and the constant fighting over drugs, Jimmy-Joe entered my life in the nick of time. Oddly enough, he too was a drug dealer -- mostly cocaine -- but while he lived with us, he made sure there was food in the refrigerator.

I was fine with it. In dysfunctional families, you take the support wherever you can find it.

But my mother's and Eddie's addictions got progressively worse after my sister was born. Mom, who was suffering from post-partum depression in addition to her normal depression, soon went from swallowing Percocet to snorting heroin. Jimmy-Joe joined her in that habit, though I never could tell who suggested it first. Then Eddie finally joined the both of them.

It was quite a trio.

The three most important people in my life, at that moment, all became heroin addicts. It was as though everybody in my life became addicted overnight. It probably had a lot to do with street economics. As I noted, a heroin habit is initially much cheaper to maintain than a pill habit.

And that's how a ninth-grade girl found herself living in what was essentially a heroin flophouse.

My weekday mornings were surreal. I woke up at six-thirty and changed into my Catholic girls' school outfit. Then I would go into the living room, stepping over strangers who were catatonic on the floor. Jimmy-Joe was usually awake already, having an early morning cigarette. He'd take me downstairs and drive me to school in whatever stolen car he had that week. Before I got out of the car, he'd hand me some lunch money.

"Be good," he'd usually say.

"I will," I replied.

Yes, he was sweet to me. Despite the fact that Jimmy-Joe was hooking up with girls my age, he never tried anything with me. In fact, he treated me like a little sister.

It wasn't just my mother, Eddie, and Jimmy-Joe. To my horror, my friend Angelica, who I went to the New Year's party with, soon became addicted to heroin too. So did several of the other kids I was hanging out with.

All around me, people were grappling with addiction.

But not me.

I continued going to classes at Nazareth Academy. I continued doing my homework. My father's warning had been burned into my mind and soul.

Thanks to my dad, as well as Jimmy-Joe, I managed to swim, not sink, through these early high school years. It's a bit of a miracle that I emerged from them without major damage.

And then came an event that was earth-shattering, even in the context of the way my family lived.

The Robbery

"They're not gonna front you any dope," said Jimmy-Joe.

My mother looked stricken, like she'd just seen a cat run over in the street. "Don't you think I fucking know that—"

We were all in the living room. I was on the couch, trying to study a textbook.

Jimmy-Joe said, "There's got to be a way for us to score another bundle."

"From where? Out of your ass?" my mother asked.

"We can get some money," he said.

My mother sighed. "But where?"

He stuck his tongue in his cheek, the way he always did when he was jonesing. "Your work."

I was in the living room with my face buried in a book, and I could only see them out of the corner of my eye. I had tried my best to ignore them, but I sure as hell couldn't ignore that.

Your work? Jesus.

"Yep," said Jimmy-Joe, now pacing between rooms, deep in thought. "But we need Mikey."

"So call him," my mother suggested.

Mikey was another guy from the neighborhood, a guy with a "reputation." He'd earned himself the nickname The Hitman after he had done a few hits for Jimmy-Joe. Yes, Mikey, "The Hitman," was actually a part of the crowd I use to hang out with. He was only three or four years older than I. He'd met Jimmy-Joe at my house. Sadly, he became addicted to heroin like many of my other friends. But I always remember Mikey being a good dancer. I loved to dance too and would always dance with him at parties.

I lifted my head and said, "You guys aren't planning to rob the hair salon, are you?"

My mother stepped into the doorway of the living room; her cheeks flushed, her eyes red-rimmed, manic. She was wearing her favorite long-sleeved purple top.

"I'm not," she said. "But him, I don't know what he's cookin' up."

"Mom—"

She interrupted me. She always did that when she knew that I was going to play the voice of conscience.

"Don't worry. We're just talking big. Ger', can I borrow $20? I promise I will give it back to you on Saturday when I get paid."

"Nope."

"Come on. I know you got a twenty. Saw it this morning."

"Not anymore."

Which was true. I used to have a twenty-dollar bill, but I'd broken it that afternoon. I was pissed my mother asked me, and I told my mother I needed the money for lunch at school for the rest of the week. But the fact was, she always paid me back.

Jimmy-Joe appeared behind her, our phone in his hand. "Hey, what day you think?" he said to Mom.

My mother turned on a dime. "Shhhh!"

Six feet away. Like I couldn't hear.

She whispered, "I'd say Tuesday mornings. Heather always lets the weekend cash just pile up in the safe till then."

Jimmy-Joe dialed a number, and he and my mother returned to the kitchen.

I slid further down into the couch and covered my face with my book. What in hell should I do? What could I do? Call the cops? Tell my father? Jesus, someone in my family was always putting me between a hammer and an anvil.

Then my mother saved me from my dilemma.

She poked her head into the living room. "Geri, don't worry. JJ's buddy says it's too dangerous. We're ditching the idea."

***

The robbery occurred the next Tuesday morning. I heard their official version after school.

According to her breathless recounting later that day, my mother had been minding her own business that morning, sweeping up around her chair, and Heather was at her desk, when these two horrible men burst through the door wearing ski masks and gloves and carrying M-16s.

One put his assault rifle to the head of the receptionist Heather and demanded that she turn over all the store's cash.

Heather was a young, attractive, petite blonde. My mother had introduced her to Jimmy-Joe prior to the robbery. The two started dating. (So, as I later figured out, Heather was in on the robbery as well.)

Obediently, Heather led him into the back room, opened her small safe with fake-palsied hands, and shoveled close to two thousand dollars into his open bag. In the meantime, my mother had stood with her hands up while the second gunman kept his gun fixed on her.

What else could I do? Guy had a frickin' M-16!

The two men sprinted out of the business and into a waiting car.

"They were just gone so fast," my mother told me from the kitchen, where she was microwaving hot dogs.

"It was a blur," said Jimmy-Joe, as though I were a complete idiot. I mean, I had heard them planning it! He was parked on our sofa, counting cash, a lot of it, into a stack on the coffee table, between a small bag of powder and the remote control.

This is so messed up, I thought, feeling pretty damned helpless. And yet, I was also enamored by Jimmy-Joe and Mike. They were such dashing criminals. Never underestimate the allure of handsome bad boys to young women.

"Love you very much," my mother said.

"If you say so," I muttered.

Jimmy-Joe gave Mikey and my mother each a stack of cash. She handed me a twenty to cover what she owed me.

Then Jimmy-Joe presented me with a few hundred dollars. "For school," he said. "And food."

Jimmy-Joe Meets His End

At this time, my cousin Ronni was the primary caregiver of my infant half-sister Dominique. Without her, I doubt that Dominique would've survived. Our home life had gotten that bad.

My father wasn't interested in intervening either. While I had some contact with him at this time, I rarely stayed the night at his place. I felt uncomfortable with his girlfriend, Diane, because she and I did not get along well. We were like oil and water. I might've carried some anger about my parents' divorce and the fact that my father had left my mother to be with her.

Meanwhile, I was dating a guy named Zac, who was three years older than I. He wasn't into heroin, thank God, but he smoked weed, drank liquor, and snorted coke (on weekends). Luckily, the more socially involved I got at my high school, the less I saw Zac and the rest of the dangerous people I considered my friends.

See, I was old enough to begin to envision a life beyond my very dysfunctional family. The problem was that my dysfunctional family was so dysfunctional that it exerted enormous gravity upon everyone and everything around it, which of course included me. I would not manage to escape that gravity for a very long time.

Meanwhile, the pressure on Jimmy-Joe was growing. There were rumors swirling that Jimmy-Joe was involved with the Russian mob. We knew for sure that he was wanted by the police for questioning. A lot of people on the street were looking at this as an opportunity to take advantage of him, because that's the type of people who run in the streets – most of them will kick a person when he's down.

Eventually, things came to a boil, and the handsome criminal who did heroin with my mother yet drove me to school and fed us decided to move out of my family's house.

"I think too many people know where I'm sleeping," he told me. "I stay here, someone's gonna rat me out, and I don't wanna go back to the joint."

We all tried to persuade him to stay, but he'd made up his mind. He packed up and left as quickly as he'd arrived.

He ended up staying in a cheap motel just outside of Philadelphia. From the day that Jimmy-Joe left, he spent the rest of his short life on the run from the police. My family stayed in touch with him because all of us had grown fond of him for different reasons.

One day, we spent hours paging and calling the motel room, but he was not responding. Eventually, Heather (who was now dating Jimmy-Joe) decided to drive out to the motel and check on him. With the manager's help, she opened the door to his room.

Jimmy-Joe was slumped over in a chair, dead at age 23.

Heroin.

At the funeral, his good friend John McMann gave the eulogy. I had never met John prior to the funeral, probably because he had been avoiding Jimmy-Joe ever since Jimmy-Joe had started using heroin, which was right around the time that we'd met him. Like Jimmy-Joe, John was seven years older than I was. He was handsome, and I had an instant schoolgirl crush on him. After Jimmy-Joe 's death, he would periodically come to my apartment to visit me, but I didn't understand why for a little while longer yet.

CHAPTER FOUR

FROM BAD TO WORSE

Baptism

My half-sister was baptized the weekend after Jimmy-Joe 's death. We had a party at the house following the baptism. My mom and her boyfriend, Eddie, were using drugs and ended up getting into a big fight in the middle of the party, which culminated with him threatening to gun down my mother using the assault rifle Jimmy-Joe had left in the house. My mother and I locked ourselves and Dominique in my bedroom for the remainder of the night.

The next day, I had to give a presentation at school. I forced myself to head to school with essentially no sleep, presented my project, and went home sick after third period.

That evening, Eddie was even higher and crazier than night before. He would drift in and out of his stupor. Each time he would come to, he'd scream about what a dump the house was and threaten to shoot my mother with Jimmy-Joe's M-16.

Once again, we hid ourselves away in the back bedroom; Eddie was too high to figure out where we were.

The next morning, I sneaked out of the bedroom. Eddie was nowhere to be seen. I presumed he had headed out to cop another bag of heroin. When I returned from school, my infant sister was asleep on the couch; my cousin Ronni watching her.

That's when Eddie burst into the house again, completely wasted. He got right back to where he had left off the day before, threatening to kill my mother. After he ranted for a while, he walked up to my mother, who looked asleep, but I'm sure was quite awake by this time, made a little gun out of his thumb and forefinger, pointed it to her head, and said, "Bang! You're going to die today!"

That was enough. I went to the next room and called the police, telling them that Eddie was threatening to kill her. The police got there fairly fast.

When Eddie saw them, he greeted them with some pleasantries. "Fuck you, pigs! I got something right here in my pants for you!"

The cops grabbed him, and since he wasn't in much shape to put up any kind of effective resistance, they soon had him handcuffed.

One of the cops asked me where the gun was. I dashed to the closet and rummaged through it, and then one of the officers took control of the M-16.

As horrible as this episode was, at least it was the last we heard of Eddie for a while. He was sent to prison for assault, terroristic threats, intent to inflict serious bodily injury, and a litany of other nasty charges. God knows it could've all been much, much worse.

***

The arc of our family story continued its downward slide. Unfortunately, my mother's addiction continued to worsen, thanks to quite a lot of enabling from others, including a few new faces. One of them was Jimmy-Joe's mother, Terri. The two of them had met at his funeral, and astonishingly the two of them began using heroin together. Terri had recently been released from prison (she had been sentenced on drug-related charges) just in time to bury her son from a heroin OD. How ironic.

The party never seemed to end at my house. Everyone was getting high. The assorted cast of characters who rotated in and out of our home were either robbing people, stealing cars, dealing other drugs, or some combination of the above to support their heroin habits.

And poor Dominique. She was only a year and a half old and had basically been abandoned by my mother. My cousin Ronni took care of her during this time, but Ronni was only sixteen years old and had issues of her own. Things grew overwhelming for her, just as they were for me.

At last, Eddie's family became concerned about the welfare of the baby. His older brother arrived with his wife one weekend to pick up Dominique, ostensibly so she could spend time with them at their house.

They never brought her back.

During this time, my mother's depression grew even worse. Finally, she sought out inpatient rehabilitation to detox from her heroin habit. It seemed to work, and she perked up for a while. This didn't last long, however. Even though she was no longer using heroin, her mental health issues were not being addressed. Untreated psychiatric illness often triggers relapse, and my mother's mental health was unstable (to say the least). I believe she struggled with, and continues to still struggle with, Major Depressive Disorder, PTSD, and severe anxiety.

She soon met a substantially older man; a contractor who was doing work on our apartment. He was probably in his mid- to late-sixties at the time. We called him Mr. Joe. He liked my mother and often loaned her money, even though she didn't reciprocate his romantic interest.

Eddie was still in prison with no possibility of release for quite a while. In an effort to get Eddie's sentence decreased, my mother asked if I would testify in court that he, in fact, did not threaten her with an assault rifle. This, of course, was a lie. I'd seen it myself.

At the time I did not want to perjure myself, but oddly enough, my mother's older sister Theresa, the aunt who often took care of me, persuaded me that doing so would help my mother. So again, I did it, knowing even as a young teenager that a free Eddie would eventually end in another disaster for us.

And I was right.

Eddie was released from prison early, of course. He and my mother found each other, of course. They both began using heroin again, of course. But what I didn't see coming was that their addictions would then grow so bad that they would completely fail to function in society.

As a result, they lost our apartment, which meant that I lost my childhood home.

This time in my life was an absolute tornado.

And then Eddie ended up violating the terms of his probation and was sent back to prison. My mother moved into a suburb of Philadelphia with Mr. Joe, the old contractor, and my baby half-sister. My cousin Ronni went back to Kensington to live with her father — my alcoholic uncle Cholly — and her disturbed sister, Amber.

And me?

I couldn't live with any of them. And I couldn't live with my father either, but it wasn't because of his condition. Financially, he appeared to be in a good place. He and Diane were running the bar, and my father was still doing masonry jobs and singing on the side. I would sometimes visit him, but I was never allowed to go outside because the neighborhood was like a war zone.

No, I couldn't live with him because I still couldn't get along with his girlfriend. Neither could he: They waged a series of ongoing battles that never seemed to get resolved. And then Diane got pregnant, giving birth to my half-brother, Bobby, in July 1995.

So, where did I go? I was just trying to get through the second half of high school so that I could escape this entire scene and move on with my life. All I needed was a stable place to live so I could accomplish it.

Two people stepped up.

Aunt Theresa and my cousin Victoria.

The same woman who'd swept me off the streets when I was four years old, helped me again when I was fifteen. Aunt Patricia lived close to my childhood home, and it was only a ten-minute car ride from my school.

But a few weeks later, I returned from a short vacation to the shore with my friends when aunt Theresa announced that I would be moving with my cousin Victoria, who lived in a suburb. She was also my godmother, and her house was close to Mr. Joe's house, where my mother was living.

It was decided.

Although I was not excited about the prospect, I was relieved to have a calm and stable place to stay.

Living with Victoria was an adjustment. She and my cousin Sal treated me as though I were a child. I don't think they fully understood that I had been taking care of myself, and to a large extent, taking care of my parents and others, since I was very young.

Furthermore, during that summer, I became close to John McMann, Jimmy-Joe's friend. Initially, I thought he was looking out for me like a little sister, but there was more to it than that, and we became romantically involved. But living under my godmother's very strict, old-school Italian rules affected my ability to openly see John, mostly because of our age difference. As a result, we stopped dating at the beginning of my junior year of high school. I kept in contact with him, but missed seeing him.

In an effort to escape the strict household rules, I began to spend weekends working with my father at his bar.

The Bar

Utter Nonsense was filled with all types of characters, from your typical barfly to your working girl and her johns, to serious addicts and assorted criminal types.

Tending bar is more art than science, and I stood there, watching my father work his magic, how he moved, how he talked, who he didn't serve. And who he did. Customers with lesions around their lips from advanced AIDS would ask to be served, and my dad never turned them away. I remember asking him once if I could wear utility gloves when I served those customers. My father explained that they were people too and that I should just wash my hands in the sterilizer fluid after serving them.

My father had gotten the bar in my mother's name despite his rap sheet and their separation. To this day, my mother believes that Dad had Diane pose as her in order to complete the application for the license, but neither my father nor Diane admitted it.

Occasionally I spent a weekend at my father's house, but it was stressful. He and Diane often fought, sometimes verbally, but also physically. He once knocked Diane's teeth out with a six-pack of beer after she had thrown a chair at him. Keep in mind, these fights would happen with my one-year-old brother Bobby present. I would take him into the bedroom while they tried to kill each other, but he was inconsolable. He would cry and wail. My mom had kept quiet after my father had hit her, but Diane kept antagonizing. These fights never seemed to end.

As my dad's drinking grew progressively worse, he and I argued more. Mostly, we quarreled about Diane; I could never understand why he had left my mother to be with her. Every negative trait he hated about my mother was ten times worse in Diane. I grew tired of arguing with him, and I didn't want to have any contact with Diane, so I stopped visiting him.

In the coming months, the relationship with my cousins also became more strained. It was hard living with them knowing that they didn't like my mother. Plus, Sal, my cousin by marriage, was the epitome of an old-school Italian, assuming the role of a king over his kingdom. In contrast, my cousin Victoria, an educated medical professional who earned the lion's share of the household income, quietly submitted to his demands.

Upon learning of the tension that had grown between my cousins and me, my mother insisted that I move in with her. I obeyed for self-serving reasons: my mother approved of my relationship with John McMann, and I would have more freedom living with my mother because her main focus was getting high.

So, one day, when my cousins went to work, I packed all my belongings and moved in with my mother and my baby sister at Mr. Joe's house.

I soon learned that my mother was upset with her family, especially her niece Victoria. When my mother's addiction began to spiral out of control, she reached out to Victoria for money. The excuse my mother gave Victoria was that she needed diapers for Dominique. Victoria declined, and with that, my mother turned very nasty. Victoria was pregnant with her first child and on bed rest. My mother made an off-hand comment to the effect of, "I hope that kid doesn't make it." Naturally, this upset my cousin, and she stopped talking to my mother.

They would not speak again. I understand that Victoria's feelings were hurt, and my mother's behavior was dead wrong. I understand that my cousin did not want to ride the roller coaster that having a relationship with my mother brings. But I have never understood how Victoria could hold a twenty-year grudge after my mother made multiple attempts to apologize.

My mother's drug use had continued mostly unabated. Despite having moments of sobriety, she was high on heroin most of her waking hours. She even had an open case with Child Services related to a call someone had made while we still lived on Garvey Drive.

I remember the caseworker visiting our home and making sure that it was clean, that there was plenty of food, and that my sister and I were taken care of. The case was closed shortly thereafter because all appeared copacetic. Of course, it wasn't. My mom was using heroin while Mr. Joe and I took care of my little sister, but the caseworker never saw any evidence of that.

I started seeing John McMann again, after it had been forbidden in my cousin's home, which made me happy. But being in a relationship with John was not always easy. He was much older than I was and able to frequent bars I couldn't get into, making it tough to spend as much time with him as I wished. He was a cocaine dealer too, and while everyone I seemed to associate with was involved in or with drugs in some form or another, I was growing sick of the drug world and everything that came with it. I wanted better for myself.

After all, one thing in my life had remained a constant, and does to this day: I seldom drink and have never fallen victim to drugs.

Release the Kraken

It was around this time that Eddie was released from prison for trying to kill my mother. Of course, their relationship was toxic. As much as she described fearing him, a part of me believes that she enjoyed the drama and the distraction from the self-inflicted problems that the relationship brought her.

The first time I saw Eddie after his release was the day he showed up drunk at Mr. Joe's house and threatened to take my sister away. I was playing with Dominique in the yard. Eddie asked for my mother, who was inside. I acted cool and collected so as not to anger him, picked up my sister, and told him that I was going to get my mother and would be right back.

Once inside the house, I locked all the doors. My mother began to panic, and it wasn't long before Eddie realized that neither my mother nor I was coming outside. He kicked and banged on the doors, threatening to kill my mother. I ran upstairs with Dominique, called the cops, and we hid in an eave.

John happened to be around that afternoon; my mother had been more permissive about seeing him than my cousin Victoria had been. John went downstairs to talk to Eddie and attempted to discourage him from coming inside. But Eddie entered the house through the back door in the kitchen. He grabbed a butcher knife and began chasing my mother around the dining room table, threatening to kill her—as usual. He ended up getting ahold of her, pinned her against the wall, and placed the knife to her throat. John intervened and got the knife out of Eddie's hand just as the police stormed into the house. They had arrived quickly.

Eddie was arrested. He'd only been out of prison for a few days!

I remember holding my baby sister and watching them push his head down into the back seat of the black-and-white cop car. As usual, Eddie resisted arrest, attempted to fight the police, was wrestled to the ground, and was handcuffed before being placed in the back seat of the patrol car. Various police officers arrived at the house, as it took multiple cops to restrain him. I remember trying my best to keep Dominique calm. What she didn't know was that it looked as though her father would be going away for a long time. To me, it was a relief, because Eddie had always genuinely frightened me.

Still, events like these often made me feel physically ill. My stomach was often in knots, my hands would sweat, and I could feel my heart beating in my throat and chest. What made this particular mess even worse was the fact that innocent little Dominique was being dragged into the middle of it.

That day, I did my best to conceal my emotions and fear so that my little sister wouldn't cry out and panic. After all, Dominique was only three years old, and she hadn't asked to be born to parents who struggled with drug addiction and severe mental health issues.

At moments like these, I often felt like an observer or outsider. I was engaging in inadvertent emotional repression, which enabled me to survive. It's not too far-fetched to compare my experience to that of a combat soldier; we both learned to respond to trauma in a manner that protects us and our fellow combatants. When besieged by incoming fire, there is little to no room for extraneous emotions, so I unconsciously dissociated from them.

This pattern has persisted and has taken a long time to break.

My Mother, the Thief

I had just started working part-time as a waitress. The first thing I usually did when I got home was stuff my tip money into my pillowcase and cover the pillow with my comforter. It wasn't to protect my stash from random burglars. It was to hide it from my mother.

I was in my senior year of high school and was actually having fun, mostly because of my girlfriends at school. Despite the dysfunction of my extended family, I had several girlfriends with whom I'm still close today. Like many girls who went to Nazareth Academy, my little gang earned our bachelor's degrees, and some of us pursued higher degrees in education, nursing, and psychology. One in particular, Sue, is the godmother to both of my children. She ended up becoming a registered nurse and is doing very well for herself.

During this time, my relationship with John McMann grew more unstable, as he realized that I was looking to attend college away from home. Still, in an effort to escape my mom and her world of drugs and drama, I would often sleep at John's house. Despite our seven-year age gap, his parents liked me and looked out for me. In fact, his mother still follows me on social media all these years later.

But my mother was my mother, and her problems would remain mine.

After meeting with my high school counselor, I decided on a list of universities to apply to. I sat down and typed out all the applications. I got the envelopes and prepaid postage ready for the letters of recommendation that a teacher had agreed to write for me.

Then the time came for me to enclose the application fee.

I went to my bed, pulled out my pillow, and reached inside the pillowcase. At last count, I had stored almost $300, which was more than enough to cover the cost of the applications.

The cash was gone.

I ransacked my room looking for the money, wondering where I could've misplaced it. But there had been no misplacement. My mother had stolen it. I knew that as surely as I knew the sun rises in the east.

I ran into the living room, where she sat watching television.

"You stole my money!" I shouted.

I watched her face closely because I could always tell when she was lying. But my mother was so zonked on heroin at that moment that she didn't even bother to lie. She just looked at me with a slack-jawed expression and then let out a little sound like huh-huh.

Whenever she was high, she would doze off, which was typical of someone on heroin. But then she'd pop awake and buzz about the house, thinking that she was accomplishing chores, such as cleaning and cooking, when in reality, she was making more of a mess.

Usually when she would steal from me, she would promise to pay it back. But in this particular instance, she really screwed me over. These applications had deadlines and it had already been down to the wire in terms of time, as I'd had to save the money.

Furious and crying, I tore out of the house and beelined for John's place. This was a breaking point—my mother had actively tried to handicap my future by stealing my college application money.

He took me into the backyard, where I emoted for what felt like hours, cursing, crying at the stars about this horrible family that the universe had saddled me with.

John's mother must've overheard us talking, because when we went back inside, she was looking at me.

She walked toward me with tears in her eyes and handed me $300 in cash. She said simply, "Please take this."

John wisely remained silent. I shifted from side to side and then finally lowered my head. "Thank you."

A few months later, despite all the challenges I faced at home, I actually graduated from high school. To my surprise, I was also accepted by all the colleges to which I had applied.

I decided to enroll at Cabrini University, where I pursued a double major in communications and Spanish. Located in the mainline section of Delaware County, Pennsylvania, the college was about thirty-five minutes from Mr. Joe's house. It was just far enough for me to get away from the craziness, yet close enough for me to come home on weekends and spend time with my little sister and friends.

But by the end of my senior year of high school, my relationship with John had grown progressively worse because he didn't want me to leave the area.

"I need to give myself a chance to achieve the life I want," I said to him.

"Why don't you want to continue that life with me?"

"Because I need to find myself first."

That was my honest reply, but he didn't like it.

John was crazy. He was a good-looking, charismatic drug dealer—kind of like my father. He came and went as he pleased, but if I so much as looked in another guy's direction, he grew insanely jealous and possessive. I think it was because he was messing around on me with other girls, and his subconscious guilt was being projected onto me. John also helped me with school tuition and prom fees. He was my prom date, despite being so much older. As much as I loved him, I had to get away from all the craziness, jealousy, and fighting that came with our relationship.

We didn't completely end our relationship at this time, but I was slowly finding my way out of it. Continuing to live at home and attend college would not have afforded me the opportunity to reach my full potential, and I wanted to finally distance myself from the drugs, illicit activities, and drama that had been so much a part of my life.

José

Nonetheless, I wasn't free yet. The summer after my graduation, one final tragedy struck.

John had finally moved out of his parents' house and into an apartment with his best friend, José, a tall, swarthy, and handsome but shy Puerto Rican. He never really did any drugs. But looking back I think he suffered from depression; I just didn't realize it at the time.

I was there the night José died in the apartment.

I had stayed over at John's apartment because the next day was Easter Sunday, and we had plans to spend the day with his family.

At three thirty in the morning, José quietly knocked on John's bedroom door. John didn't wake up, so I went to the door instead. José was distraught over a breakup with his girlfriend and stated that he had done heroin to numb the pain. I knew the guy was high on heroin just by looking at his eyes—remember my hard-won experience—but he wasn't nodding off nor incoherent.

I did my best to reassure José that he would recover from the breakup. He stated that he wanted to leave the apartment and drive over to his ex-girlfriend's apartment to talk to her. I told him that he shouldn't risk driving in his condition, and I expressed concern about his safety. He agreed, saying that he would finish his beer and go to bed instead. We talked for about half an hour, and I went back to John's room exhausted.

John and I woke up at around 7 a.m. John left the bedroom, and I was still getting dressed when he began to scream at the top of his lungs.

I ran out into the living room and saw José sitting on the couch with his feet up on the coffee table; he was in the same position I had left him in when we had spoken only hours before. His glassy eyes stared vacantly ahead, and his body looked rigid.

He was dead.

Nonetheless, I grabbed the phone and called 911. John was hysterical and unable to perform CPR successfully on José. I spoke with the 911 operator, who asked me to implement a different CPR technique on José because he was still unresponsive. I pushed John out of the way and began to press on José's breastbone while pushing air into his lungs. At one point, I thought I heard him breathing, but it turned out it was just me pushing the air in and out of his lungs.

The paramedics arrived, but José remained unresponsive.

He died Easter morning, 1999.

I remember having to stay in the apartment and wait for the coroner to arrive and take José away. It felt very surreal, as if I were an observer looking in on a terrible tragedy that was taking place around me.

José had had no money, and his adoptive father had passed away several months prior to his death. John held a fundraiser in an attempt to provide his friend with a proper funeral service. It was successful, and John had a memorial service for José and had him cremated.

José was only twenty-six years old.

Once again, I disconnected from my emotions so that I was able to make sensible decisions under stress. What still bothers me about José's death is that I am unsure as to whether it was intentional. I've thought, "I should have talked with him longer. Maybe if I had, he would not have died that night."

Falling once again into a self-protective mode of managing the trauma and sadness associated with José's tragic death, I relied on intellect for comfort and self-assurance. It is true that if I had stayed up that night and talked with José until morning, he might have lived to see Easter Sunday. Yet, I also realize that José had been heading down a self-destructive path and using heroin to cope. Is it realistic for me to think that I could have saved him every time he used heroin? No, because none of us can stop or save someone from addiction—not without the addicted person taking on most of the responsibility for getting clean. You can suggest, recommend, and offer help, but ultimately, the decision is not up to a person on the outside. The decision is up to the individual who is struggling with this disease.

That spring, as I continued my freshman year of college, I carried with me the hope that I was taking the first step toward making a brand-new life for myself.

But there is a famous phrase—if you want to make God laugh, tell Him your plans.

CHAPTER FIVE

SISTER GERI GROWS UP

Strange Code of Ethics

During my college years, I didn't talk to my father. A wedge had driven itself between us, and its name was alcohol.

My mother would hear things about him from my cousins and update me on his crazy life. I even remember coming home to Mr. Joe's house one day and finding my mother cutting my father's hair in my bedroom. He was drunk, and she was high on heroin. I called Diane to come pick him up, but I didn't say much to him or to any of them at the time.

Honestly, it was as if my dad was a different person. The dad who had instilled morals in me regarding family and education no longer existed. He was consumed by his own addiction to alcohol.

I also learned that in addition to drinking heavily, my father had begun to manufacture and distribute methamphetamine again. He was cooking meth in the basement of his bar.

Through the grapevine, I eventually learned that his alcohol abuse had spiraled out of control and that he had ended up seeking help from his family doctor in order to detox. Diane later shared with me that he was experiencing visual hallucinations. For example, she once found him on his hands and knees, pounding his slipper against the floor, complaining about imaginary bugs that were crawling all over the house.

From a clinical perspective, alcohol withdrawal is among the most difficult titration and detox processes. While withdrawing from alcohol, it is quite common to experience hallucinations in addition to possible seizures, hand tremors, and loss of equilibrium.

Meanwhile, my father's bar was robbed at gunpoint a number of times. It wasn't necessarily for money, I learned. Instead, this was how the drug dealers retaliated against him for not allowing them to deal heroin and crack cocaine out of his bar. I guess, according to his code of ethics, it was okay for him to cook meth in the basement of his bar, but it was not okay to deal other types of drugs.

Off the Deep End

Throughout all of this, my mother's addiction to heroin continued to grow out of control. She often woke up at 5 a.m. to steal money from me or Mr. Joe. If that didn't work, she would tell some extravagant lie to extract cash from Mr. Joe.

During my college years, in addition to dope, my mother was actively taking a slew of other substances, such as non-prescribed benzodiazepines. Specifically, she got hooked on Xanax and Valium.

Eventually, the combination of heroin and other substances put my mother in a drug-induced psychosis. The best way to describe what drug-induced psychosis looks like is to imagine someone experiencing a bad trip from LSD.

My mother's psychosis began one sunny May weekend when I came home from college to work, study for finals, and spend time with my little sister. Mr. Joe had become Dominique's primary caregiver while I'd been away at school. I also had friends who lived in the area. These friends hadn't gone away to college and would sometimes help Mr. Joe by taking Dominique to dance class or to the playground. My mother was not in the picture as a caregiver. She couldn't even care for herself.

When I walked in the door, I found my mother in the middle of the living room floor holding a frying pan and a batch of whole, raw potatoes. She was mumbling, and her speech was incoherent. She was saying things such as, "The fucking cops are here, and they're going to fucking get me."

I called my good friend "Slim" and asked him if he could help me get my mother into the car, so I could get her to the hospital. When Slim arrived, my mother initially thought he was a police officer and that we were trying to arrest her. We went along with that delusion and asked her to come out to the police car.

She leaned over and whispered into my ear, "Don't let them get my fucking dope."

We took her to the hospital, and she was later transported to a psychiatric facility.

A few days later, I got a call from the center; the clinical team wanted to meet with Mr. Joe and me. We sat down with them, and the doctors said that they had been unsuccessful in helping my mother return to a "normal" mental state. They asked about Dominique and instructed me to ensure that the appropriate guardianship/custody arrangements were made regarding her care because they believed that my mother had suffered permanent brain damage and doubted that she would ever return to baseline functioning.

I was in shock. I asked if I could see her, and they hesitantly agreed.

When I arrived on the ward, I glimpsed my mother running up and down the hallway naked with a staff member chasing her and trying to dress her. They wouldn't let me help and made me wait to see her.

After what felt like an eternity, a staff member finally escorted me to see my mother. They had succeeded in dressing her. She was sitting in a wheelchair, and her wrists and ankles were restrained.

The clinician leaned over to her. "Do you know who this is?"

She looked up at me. "That's one of my Jerry's girlfriends."

My mother then reared back, spat on me, dropped her chin to her chest, and started mumbling to herself.

The staff members escorted me out of the room. I remember sitting in my car and crying. I then contacted my aunts to tell them about my mother's state of mind.

It was the end of the academic year for me, so I came home for the summer to work as a waitress. I was concerned that I might not be able to return to college due to my mother's mental health; I thought I might have to stay home and take on more responsibility by caring for my sister.

About two weeks after my horrific visit to see my mother, the phone rang.

"Hello?" I said.

"Geri-Lynn, get me the fuck out of here!"

It was my mother. I didn't care that she was upset about being in a psychiatric hospital. I was happy to hear her voice, however shrill, but I wasn't going to go check her out of there until I thought she was ready. Turns out, she didn't need me to do it for her.

She hung up on me and then had herself discharged. Mr. Joe went and picked her up while I watched Dominique. And no sooner had she walked in the door than she was on her way out again to score heroin.

John and I also ended our four-year relationship around this time. It had petered out of its own natural accord. We remained friendly, and I still saw him on occasion. Although being in a relationship with John was like riding a wild roller coaster, he and his family always had my best interests at heart.

Mr. Joe

While I was at Mr. Joe's home one weekend, he suffered a stroke. I remember being awakened by the sound of his voice, downstairs, apparently on the phone, attempting to say that something was wrong with him. His speech was slurred and fragmented.

I ran downstairs, grabbed the phone from him, and realized that he was talking to a 911 operator. I asked the operator to send an ambulance. After it arrived and took him away, I woke Dominique and got her ready for day care.

After dropping her off, having kept her blissfully ignorant of what was happening, I floored it over to the hospital and told them that I was Mr. Joe's granddaughter. They asked me to sign release papers for tissue plasminogen activator (TPA), also known as the clot-buster medication, because it breaks up blood clots that are commonly associated with strokes.

As it became clear that Mr. Joe was facing a long recovery, I needed to make plans for Dominique. Neither of my aunts would agree to care for her. My best friend Sue's mom, Jeanette, was single and a nurse. I asked her if she would be willing to take care of my sister in the fall so that I could return to school. An angel in human form, Jeanette agreed, and Dominique moved into Sue and Jeanette's house in late August.

By this time, Eddie was clean, sober, and out of prison once again. He contacted me and asked if he could see his daughter, perhaps even take her for a weekend. I reluctantly agreed. This upset me because I did not want him to see her, but my aunt Theresa encouraged me to let him. Remember, she is also the one who asked me to testify in court that he had not threatened my mother's life so that he could get out of jail. I should have trusted my gut. What kills me, even more, is that she wasn't even the one taking care of Dominique or me, and yet she had these opinions regarding Eddie and my mother!

One weekend, Eddie took my sister for a visit and never brought her back.

I was crushed.

At this point, my mother decided to go into rehab. She completed rehab and moved into a halfway house. After Eddie took my sister, my mother and Eddie ended up seeing each other again. Both clean and sober, they dated for several months.

However, my mother had no custody arrangement; she had assumed that because they were back together, it wasn't necessary. My mom and

Eddie stopped seeing each other after a few months. Just like that, Eddie told my mother that she was no longer allowed to see her daughter, who was five years old at the time, because he no longer wanted to see my mother. He began seeing another woman. Her name was Sandy, and she was his best friend Steve's sister. Dominique absolutely loathed her.

I spent time and money hiring a lawyer on my mother's behalf to try to get her visitation rights to see my sister. This went on for five years—until my sister was nearly ten years old.

Graduation

I graduated with honors from Cabrini University in May 2002. I basically had no home to return to, so I moved into an apartment with my friend Nasir. He was a friend of Slim, whom I had gotten to know at my waitressing job. Both were from Palestine, and I grew close to them. They were quite aware of my family situation, and many nights, I would sleep at their apartment. There were even times when I earlier borrowed money from them to pay my college tuition.

Just prior to graduating from college, I landed a job in advertising, working for a guy named Duke. He owned multiple tanning salons that were part of a large franchise located in the northeast of the country. Therefore, my first job out of college was creating and developing advertising campaigns for his tanning salons.

Through working for Duke, I met many radio and television consultants in the Philadelphia market. Before long, one of them offered me a job at a Top 40 radio station. I accepted and quickly worked my way up the ranks, becoming a successful sales representative.

After many years of friendship, Nasir and I became romantically involved. His family owned a Moroccan restaurant in Philadelphia, and they ran a shady Arabic nightclub out of the basement. I often tended bar there on the weekends after working as a radio sales rep during the week.

Overall, things seemed to be going quite well for me. My mom was still living in a halfway house and doing well. My father, however, was a different story. I hadn't talked to him in years—not since my mother had descended into the depths of heroin addiction.

I sat down and wrote a letter to my father, telling him that I was the first Utter to graduate from college. I told him that I had managed to do it without his financial support or any physical or emotional help. But, I also let him know that what had helped me get through college and all the other challenges in my life (which he had been oblivious to) had been my recollection of our talks during my childhood and of how much faith he'd had in me and my abilities. Though we didn't talk, I still had a strong desire to make him proud. Talk about the amount of power and influence a person can have on someone, even when they are not around! I asked him to call me and gave him my number.

He did call me, and after many years, we reconnected. It turned out that he was still with Diane. In addition to my little brother, Bobby, they had a little girl named Brittany Lee, whom they called Lee-Lee.

Most importantly, he had stopped drinking.

I agreed to meet them for dinner. From that point on, my father and I began to see each other regularly. With the exception of his being with Diane, he was back to being the dad that I remembered as a little girl.

Progress

My advertising/radio sales career was very successful. In that field, when you are good at selling, other competitive radio stations reach out and offer you opportunities and substantial pay increases to work with them. One year out of college, I was making nearly $60,000 a year. This jumped to six figures over the next few years.

Although I enjoyed being with Nasir, our romance didn't work out. My dad liked him, partly because Nasir had been a biochemist, and they had attempted to make phencyclidine, better known as PCP or angel dust, together. They intended to distribute it, which I reminded them was a clear violation of the law, but I allowed them to do their thing and stayed out of it. Although Nasir was a bright guy, he was a little bit of a gangster and was always looking for a way to make a quick buck. Luckily, the PCP venture didn't work out. Nasir and I went our separate ways. He ended up getting into medical school and becoming a doctor. Go figure.

Every couple of months, my dad would call me when he was fighting with Diane. He would ask me to come pick him up from the city so he could stay at my house, and I would always oblige. He would come to my house, stay for a couple of days, and then go back to Diane and the kids. I served as a steam safety valve on the boiler of his life.

During this time, my dad started drinking again. He would throw back Canadian Windsor on the rocks at night before bed. As much as I hated his backsliding, I found a false sense of comfort in telling myself that he was drinking only at night.

My mom was doing well, having had only a few relapses here and there.

With the help of a lawyer, I was still trying to get visitation rights to Dominique. I finally began to make some headway. The truth was that I knew exactly where my sister lived, but I didn't feel comfortable going there and attempting to see her. I was afraid of Eddie—and with damned good reason.

Gathering up my courage, I called him one day. Eddie was surprisingly courteous. I asked if I could see her. I couldn't believe his answer: "No problem."

Soon, I found myself taking Dominique out for shopping trips to the mall in the afternoons, buying clothes, eating lunch, and laughing at stupid movies.

Eddie still would not let my mother see her, and this severely upset my mom. I never liked to see either of my parents upset, even when they were clearly responsible for their miserable actions. For this reason, I continued to push the lawyer to help my mother get visitation rights to my sister.

Pasquale

During one of my mother's stints in rehab, she met a man named Pasquale—Pat for short—and they quickly started a relationship. He had a long criminal background and had once been found guilty of armed robbery, which had ended in an eleven-year state prison sentence.

After his release from prison, he'd married a young woman who was nearly twenty years his junior, and they'd had two sons.

While in rehab, Pasquale was going through a divorce, When I would go up to visit my mother on weekends, I would see Pasquale, and I thought he was a really nice guy—you know . . . all things considered.

When they both got out of rehab, they lived in separate sober-living houses for a while before moving in together.

Oddly enough, they moved into an apartment in my complex, making us neighbors. Pasquale worked as a roofer and a barber, and my mother began to cut hair part-time again.

We finally went to court, and my mother gained weekend visitation with my sister.

Dominique began coming to my mother's apartment on weekends, and we all hung out and looked like a "normal" family. Moreover, my parents would actually talk when my dad came to my apartment; he even got along with Pasquale!

In December 2004, after a long night out with friends, my mother barged into my apartment and told me that my beloved Mommom had passed away.

She had experienced a cardiac arrest and passed away at the nursing home where she lived. Memories of Mommom flooded my brain. While Mommom lived at the nursing home, I would pick her up on weekends, bring her to my house, and have her teach me all the old Italian recipes that she used to prepare for me when I was a kid. We cooked everything from homemade fettuccine Alfredo to pasta fagioli.

Needless to say, I took her death pretty hard and miss her still.

Dominique

One evening, I got home late from the radio station after a long day of listening to self-involved business owners trying to hustle me for cheaper air time, a date, or both. As soon as I plopped down on the couch and kicked my heels off, my phone started ringing off the hook. I saw that it was my mother's number and didn't answer immediately; I just assumed that she wanted to bother me about something as usual.

Just when I decided that I had enough energy to make it into a bath, my doorbell rang. I peeked out the balcony window and saw Dominique, who was visibly upset. I thought about what an adorable kid she was. Slim with shoulder-length blonde hair and blue eyes, she looked very much like her father. With my olive skin, dark hair, and dark eyes, I looked much more like my mother.

I had a pretty good idea of what was going on. My mother had only recently gained full custody of my little sister. If she was showing up in this kind of shape, it meant that my mother was probably off the rails. Again.

I ran down the steps to let her in.

As she rushed inside crying, she blurted out, "Mommy and Pat are getting high. I don't want to be around them. I snuck out. I don't know what to do, Ger!"

And damn, I got pissed. I was so sick of this. I had lived it my whole life, and now I was seeing it happen to another child.

"Stay here," I ordered. "Don't answer the door. Don't answer the phone. I'll be back soon. You got that?"

With tears streaming down her face, Dominique nodded.

I gave her a hug and whispered that it would be okay, though I didn't believe it myself. I slipped my shoes back on and headed over to my mother's.

When I got there, I peeked through the sliding screen doors and saw both of them nodding off on the couch. The apartment was filthy, and the phone had been yanked out of the wall—presumably to make sure that Dominique couldn't call to tell me they had been using. Again.

I burst inside. But they were both so under the influence that they barely acknowledged my presence. There had been many times that I'd wanted to punch my mother in the face, and this sure as hell was one of them.

"What in God's name is the matter with you, Mom?" I screamed. "You just got custody of Dominique, and you're already high? How can you do this? What the hell is wrong with you? What is wrong with you?"

Obviously, I couldn't answer that, and neither could my mother. The best I could do was put my nose an inch away from hers and scream my head off about what a terrible mother, a horrible person, and a pathetic drug addict she was. In a rather lame attempt to appear as if I had violent tendencies to back up my words, I kicked over a few dining room chairs.

Then, crying, I stormed out. I knew that if I did not take Dominique, she would end up in the system as a ward of the state. I was only twenty-five years old, was at the height of my successful advertising career, and was having a hell of a good time to boot. I knew that I would now become a surrogate mother to a ten-year-old. I wasn't unhappy about it, just scared to death.

I've been working on this book for nearly two years, the bulk of which covered the first two decades of my life. But since I began writing, there hasn't been a hiatus in the stress that I endure from those around me who suffer from drug addiction, or from those fellow loved ones who suffered collateral damage alongside me, family members like Dominique.

In writing this book, I have shared with you what my relationship has been like with my half-maternal sister. During the first ten years of Dominique's life, I was actively involved in her care. So much so that I made sure that I attended a local college so that I could spend time with her on the weekends while monitoring my mother and how she cared for my sister when also using heroin.

Although I was born into a chaotic family, to unstable parents, at times, I experienced what I perceived to be normalcy. Granted, my definition is probably severely skewed compared to that of the general population; still, I feel as though my parents made more of an intentional effort to care for me and show me love, whereas any love that my sister experienced from her father, Eddie, and my mother was even more disjointed and dysfunctional.

The task of raising Dominque was now in my hands. Raising a ten-year-old adolescent girl with severe abandonment issues was emotionally and psychologically exhausting. As much as I wanted to help my sister, I also harbored feelings of resentment for my mother and her father, as clearly it shouldn't have been my responsibility to raise my sister. But I knew that if I didn't step in, my sister would end up in the foster care system. And that was the last thing I wanted for her.

So Dominique moved into my apartment. Because I didn't want my sister to be a latchkey kid, and I wanted her to feel safe in my home, I hired an old-school Italian nanny to cook for her and to be there when she arrived home from school. This worked well until my Italian nanny started to experience health issues after she was with us for about a year.

This was just around the time that my father and Diane parted ways, and my father had nowhere to live. He asked if he could live with me and I reluctantly agreed. So I now had my ten-year-old sister and my fifty-something father living in my apartment. Not exactly the salad days I had imagined for that point in my life. But I had to find a way to embrace the situation and make it advantageous for everyone.

Naturally, I asked my father to help me raise Dominique. He did so without hesitation, and having him around helped me manage my sister's behaviors. When I initiated the foster care and adoption process for my sister, Dominique, my father played an integral role in interacting and interfacing with Children and Youth Services. So much so that in all of the original paperwork, both he and I were referred to as her foster parents.

Don't get me wrong, Dominique was still a huge pain and did the best she could to test her limits; But now she saw a positive male role model in her life who actually cared, and his presence and the kind, yet firm, way he interacted with her helped to improve some of her acting-out. And feeling needed helped my father.

My dad never missed a beat when my sister tried to pull one over on him. For instance, on one occasion, I took her cell phone away. While I was at work, she sneaked into my bedroom, grabbed the phone, and returned to her room so she could call her friends. No sooner had she closed her door, than my father gently pushed it opened and, without saying a word, put his hand out for the phone. She handed it over.

She never argued or talked back to him. On the other hand, she perceived me as her emotional punching bag. I feel as though, perhaps because I was trying to offer her a stable life, she felt safe, and in a strange way, that safeness evoked fear in her. Fear that I would abandon her like my mother and her father. That old saying, "No good deed goes unpunished," is my mantra for my relationship with my sister.

Greg

After a few years of being single and having a blast, I met my husband on December 28, 2005.

When Greg walked into the restaurant, I was distracted by a basketball game on the television. This handsome, blue-eyed, dark-haired guy started to talk to me. He asked me which high school I went to. I later learned this was his opening line for chatting to everyone.

Before I knew it, he was in my car trying to get some action. I told him that if he was interested in me, he would ask me out on a proper date. The next day, he called and asked me out on a date that Saturday night. We would end up dating, falling in love and were married on April 18, 2010.

Greg is a junior-high school physical education teacher. Prior to completing his master's in education, he traveled the country, playing basketball for the New York Nationals against the Harlem Globetrotters. The youngest of three boys, he was raised in an upper-middle-class family.

But when we started dating, Greg and his family knew little about my family's sordid history.

I was hesitant to share with Greg that I took care of my sister full-time and that the rest of my family was batshit crazy. So, I revealed these things to him in small doses. I was afraid that if I told him everything all at once, he would run for the hills. Instead, Greg did the exact opposite: he accepted my sister as if she were his own.

His mother, on the other hand, had a tougher time accepting my lunatic family. But, hey, can you blame her?

Mr. Mom

My dad continued to be "Mr. Mom." He cooked, went food shopping, cleaned, managed the bills (with my money!), fixed things around the apartment, and helped me raise my sister.

My family was hip to milking the system. Because I was financially supporting my sister on my own, Dad suggested that I try to adopt her. By doing that, I would receive medical and cash benefits for her, as well as access to different resources.

I took his advice and was able to get my sister in-home therapy services and her own insurance. I also received a cash stipend every month to help care for her. But during this time, I was financially supporting my father and his children. In many ways, my dad thrived when he lived with me. He was happy and felt like he had a purpose taking care of the household and helping me with my sister. He also had a very vibrant social life and even began singing with the Destinations again after a decade-long hiatus. But I also felt as though I enabled him by giving him money. Like all the women in his life, I supported him financially, so the cycle continued. But I was just happy to have a close relationship with my dad again.

Oddly enough, my father became Dominique's foster father, and she called my dad "F-Squared or F²" for "foster father."

My dad would also bring my little brother Bobby and his little sister to my apartment on weekends. My three younger half-siblings all hung out together. At the time, Dominique was twelve, Bobby was eleven, and Lee-Lee was five.

We had a pretty good system going for a while, I think. I financially supported everyone, and my dad took care of all of us. Even when my mom would get busted and end up in jail or rehab, my dad would be the one to go visit her, put money on her books in jail, and ask her and Pasquale if they needed anything.

I continued progressing in my career and signed a contract as a national advertising sales consultant for AccuWeather.com.

It was also around this time that I applied to the master's program in clinical and counseling psychology at Chestnut Hill College. I attended the program part-time, worked full-time, and earned my degree in August of 2011. I then applied to one doctoral program. They accepted only fifteen to twenty students in each cohort, and Sister Geri was one of them! I then earned my doctorate in clinical psychology.

Losing My Dad

That summer, my sister and I moved into Greg's house, and my father moved into an apartment complex that was within walking distance. I missed having my dad around, but I also understood that, for the sake of my upcoming marriage, it was time for my dad to move out. Greg, like the incredible man that he is, picked right up where my father had left off. He stepped in and was just as invested in my sister's future as I was.

Things went well for a while. My dad had a beautiful apartment (that I paid for), and he continued to cook dinner and help out around my house so that I could invest my time in work and school.

In the spring of 2010, my dad began to complain of lower back pain that shot up into his shoulder. I took him to his primary care physician, who referred him to a gastroenterologist, who diagnosed him with pancreatitis and an infected gallbladder.

Dad's two younger children and Diane had been living in the mountains when Diane had a falling out with the landlord. Since they had nowhere else to go, my dad asked her and the kids to move in with him. So, it was my father, Diane, Bobby, and Lee-Lee living in a one-bedroom apartment on my dime. Although Diane and I had a rocky past, it was a good thing that she and the kids were living with my dad; as his health continued to decline, Diane took care of him.

After my wedding, my dad underwent surgery to have his gallbladder removed, but his condition worsened rather than improved. Multiple specialists told us that he had a nasty case of pancreatitis and advised him to stop drinking alcohol and smoking cigarettes. My father was in so much pain that he actually listened. He lost nearly forty pounds in the ensuing weeks.

On the Fourth of July weekend in 2010, my father was so sick that Greg and I rushed him to the hospital, where he was diagnosed with stage IV pancreatic cancer. The doctor told him that he had six months to live. My father discharged himself from the hospital, and several days later, we placed him in in-home hospice care.

I remember when the doctor came in to deliver the dismal prognosis to my father. He started by explaining that it was, in fact, pancreatic cancer that had metastasized. My father wasn't one to complain much. Leading up to the weekend, he had been vomiting, moaning, and doubled over in severe pain. Once he was admitted to the hospital, I remember him being on IV morphine. He was also receiving bolus doses of Dilaudid but was still in so much pain. Prior to his admission to the hospital, a pain management doctor had prescribed OxyContin and morphine pills, so by the time he was admitted to the hospital, his tolerance was very high. The doctor continued to talk for what felt like forever. He recommended chemotherapy.

At that point, my father put his hand out, making a stopping motion as if he were shushing him. He looked the young doctor in the face and said, "Doc, is the chemo gonna save my life?"

The doctor began to stutter. "It may prolong your life, Mr. Utter."

My father threw up his hands. "How much time do I have left if I don't do the chemo?"

This time, the doctor grew emotional, and his bottom lip trembled. "Maybe six months, Mr. Utter."

My father looked at me, Diane, and the doctor. "Then get me out of here. I am not spending the time I have left in this fucking hospital!"

The following day, he was discharged to home hospice.

My mother was doing well around this time and she would sit with Diane at my dad's apartment to keep her company. Unfortunately, her sobriety wouldn't last, but this was a nice gesture while she was up to it.

I visited my dad every day; the sicker he became, the more difficult it was for me to see him like that. Dominique and Dad's two younger children would also spend a lot of time with him.

A chaplain came to his apartment and prayed with him. He was suffering from what's referred to as terminal agitation, which can best be described as an individual feeling as though their work here on Earth is not done, and they, therefore, won't surrender to the dying process because they feel there is more to accomplish or that they must make amends with others.

During the last days of August, my father became incoherent. Diane told me that one of the last things he shared with her was a dream he'd had of a little boy standing under a tree. He believed that little boy was my unborn child. I was indeed pregnant, but it was too early for an ultrasound.

On September 3rd at around 6 p.m., I took all the kids to the local mall for an outing. My friend Sue, who was a nurse, visited my dad, mom, and Diane at my dad's apartment. While Sue was checking my dad's heart rate and pulse, he passed away. My mother called shortly after to tell me. That was one of the most difficult calls I've ever received, not simply because my father had died—believe me, that was hard enough—but because I had all three kids with me in a public place. I decided to load them back into the car and head back to the apartment.

I remember driving back to the apartment knowing that my father was dead and not sharing it with the kids in the car because I didn't know how I would manage all of their emotions; it would have to wait until we were home.

The undertaker came to the house and removed my father's body. It felt like something out of a movie, but I also felt a great sense of relief. He had suffered for such a long time that I don't think any of us could have borne watching him suffer any longer.

At the funeral, my dad's group, the Destinations, sang around his coffin, and I gave the eulogy.

Dominique took my father's passing just as hard as his biological children, myself included. They had grown close over the four years that he helped raise her. She saw him as her protector. She recalled a time when Eddie, mad at our mother, made nasty threats to my sister over the phone. Without hesitation, my father went down to Eddie's house on Auburn Street, located in the heart of the Badlands and walking distance from Utter Nonsense, knocked on the door, and read him the riot act for harassing a ten-year-old girl.

I experienced feelings of great loss and sadness at my father's passing. Some who know how dysfunctional and downright criminal my family was may wonder why my love for him never faded throughout the years of turmoil and danger. But in fact, when he wasn't in the grips of his addiction, he could be charming, funny, and a true force of nature—someone who drew all of those around him into his orbit. It was he who had protected me at times, in his own way. It was he who had insisted that I was different from the rest of the drug-addled members of my family. It was he who had nurtured in me the sense not to get high. Most of all, it was he who had convinced me that I would grow up to be successful and happy.

Around Thanksgiving 2010, I went for an ultrasound and learned that I was indeed having a boy! My father's dream had been prescient. My husband had promised my father that should we have a boy, we would name him Gregory Jerome; giving him my husband's first name and my father's middle name.

Life, as they say, found a way to renew itself after my father's death.

Another Relapse

Unfortunately, the inevitable happened, and Mom and Pat relapsed. As much as I wanted to hate them for it, I had learned by this point that it wouldn't make a difference. So, I controlled what I felt I could, and that was ensuring that my sister had somewhat of a decent shot at a normal life.

Throughout their fifteen-plus-year relationship, my mother and Pat had good times—or times of significant sobriety—and not-so-good times, when they would relapse and end up in jail or rehab. For the longest time, I had the perception that this was their choice; they chose to be junkies. And because they chose that over their children, I was livid. However, it was also around this time that I thought I needed somebody to talk to. I was at the height of my career in advertising, which was exciting but filled with pressure, a lot of which was self-induced because I always wanted to do well. Mix that with raising a ten-year-old who had a bunch of emotional issues related to feeling that she was unlovable because her parents had made life so hard for her. It felt good just to talk to somebody who wasn't a family member, because family members always had opinions and felt that they could say derogatory things about my mother. Even though my aunts are my mother's sisters, talking about her in what I perceived to be a derogatory manner was off-limits. The only person who could speak ill of my mother was me. If anyone talked badly about her, I immediately came to her defense, and I still do. I wanted to dig a little deeper within myself to understand why my mother had done the things she'd done. I thought if I gained an understanding, this would allow me to be empathetic. It was also around this time that I began to kick around the idea of returning to school for psychology. But that wouldn't come for several more years—not until I met Dr. Howard Cohen.

At twenty-three years old, I started seeing psychologist, Dr. Cohen. He treated me off and on for about ten years and helped to validate my feelings about my mother and other family members. He was nurturing in a way that I desperately needed. He listened to me while affording me the opportunity to learn more about myself. He helped me realize what I wanted out of life. His office was one of the only places where I felt comfortable enough to cry and let it all out. He also gave me permission to give myself a break. He taught me to be kind to myself while offering support and generous encouragement to pursue an advanced degree in psychology. I wonder if clinicians like Dr. Cohen realize the positive impact they can have on a person. However, since becoming a doctor myself, I have experienced reassurance when I run into old patients who share with me how much I helped them during a pivotal time in their lives.

To protect myself and my sister, I took a new approach when it came to my interactions with my mom. I told her that I would help her anytime day or night if she would help herself. And by help herself, I meant going into rehab to treat her addiction. I was done lending her money and listening to the elaborate lies and stories she told in her efforts to get money out of me. My mother had been suffering from opioid addiction for roughly ten years at this point, and I had learned what her lies looked and sounded like before they even came out of her mouth. I had also learned about the patterns of behavior that I had begun to observe when it came to her relapsing, being on the brink of a relapse, or being actively addicted. At times, it was difficult to deny my mother money to feed her addiction, because I knew what she was doing to support her habit—for example, stealing from department or grocery stores. It was difficult for me to not give her money because I did not want to see her go to jail. However, she eventually went to jail for retail theft and drug possession. This was difficult for me to watch because nobody wants to see others suffer, especially their parents.

I'm sharing all of this with you to convey that for me to continue to love my mother, I had to change the way I perceived her. And the person who played an integral role in my being able to still love my mom was my father. When she and Pasquale relapsed and I took my sister, my dad hadn't started living with me yet. We would talk a lot on the phone, and no matter how frustrated I was with my mother, he would listen and help me find a solution or a way to potentially help her. It wasn't until he moved in with me and learned exactly how bad my mom's addiction was that he and I began to talk about it. And to this day, I really think he harbored a significant amount of guilt for my mother's addiction because she did not start to use opioids until after they separated. So, I feel as though he shared the burden of her addiction out of guilt. I also observed patterns in my father regarding the women he ended up with. His mother was a tortured soul who was both the victim and the perpetrator of significant physical abuse. My mother was the victim of significant trauma in her household, and Diane was the victim of significant physical and domestic violence. My father, being a victim of physical and verbal abuse himself, was attracted to people who were similar to him but, at the same time, psychologically weaker than he was. His understanding of my mother's struggles allowed him to teach me empathy.

I remember very clearly an occasion when my mother had relapsed and ended up in jail. I was so enraged. My dad and I were taking care of Dominique, and she called from jail, crying. I was ready to cut her off and not help her. However, my dad turned to me, and he said, "Look, kid, I know you are mad at your mother. She can be the biggest junkie in the world, but she is still your mother. You only get one. I know you may not think it or feel it, but your mother loves you more than anything in the world. She's just sick."

That's when the lightbulb went on for me, and I began to view her addiction as an illness or a disease and not a choice. Because who wants to live like the junkie she was? She was a tortured soul, and I couldn't think of anyone under any circumstances who would choose to live a tortured life. That's when I really learned about empathy.

Through all of this, Pat and my mom stayed together. Everyone—even my dad—liked Pat despite his issues and his struggle with addiction. Whether he was in jail or out of jail or rehab or he was doing well, I had a soft spot for Pasquale. Unlike my dad and Eddie, Pasquale was always respectful toward my mother. When you're married to a gigolo like my father for as long as my mother was, you have significant trust issues. Pat bore the brunt of some of those trust issues with patience and perseverance. Pat and my mom sincerely loved each other.

In 2010, Pat went to the doctor and was diagnosed with hepatitis C. Apart from experiencing more fatigue than usual, he felt fine. But his physician noticed that his calves were swollen and discolored and decided to run some tests on his liver. So, Pat embarked on a journey to get treatment for hepatitis C at Jefferson Hospital. He participated in a clinical trial and was free of hepatitis C after about sixteen weeks. The hepatitis left significant scarring of the liver, also known as cirrhosis. A hepatologist at Jefferson Hospital continued to monitor him. Pat would undergo fairly regular imaging. They wanted to monitor him for any potential occurrence of cancer, as the rate of liver cancer is higher among those who have hepatitis C and cirrhosis.

In or around 2012, Pat violated the terms of his probation and was sent back to county jail. The violation consisted of a urine test that was positive for heroin. This was one of the times when he and my mother relapsed.

While in jail, Pat shared with the medical staff that he was under the care of doctors for continued liver monitoring and treatment. Ultrasound imaging taken in jail revealed that he had a 6 cm mass in his liver. Pat had gone to high school with the chief of adult probation in Montgomery County, Pennsylvania, Mike Gordon. Over the years, whenever Pat would get into any kind of legal trouble and end up in the county jail, Mike would always help him out. When Pat received word that there were masses in his liver, Mike helped to expedite his release so that he could continue undergoing medical treatment.

In 2016, Pat decided to get a medical opinion at the Hospital of the University of Pennsylvania. The doctors believed that the masses were benign; however, they wanted to continue to monitor Pat. During this time, he was asymptomatic, healthy, and active. In 2017, the masses began to grow, indicating that they were, in fact, cancerous. Pat underwent transarterial chemoembolization (TACE), in an attempt to keep the masses small so that he could meet the criteria for a liver transplant. At that time, he met all the inclusion criteria for a liver transplant.

In 2017, Pat and my mom were using heroin on an inconsistent basis. They tended to use it at the start of the month, which was when they received their disability checks. By mid-month, they would put themselves back on buprenorphine, using it as a bridge between illicit heroin and sobriety. Between the time that Pat was on the liver transplant list, and when he no longer met the criteria, he received two calls. These calls were from the hospital, notifying him of a donor match. Each time, he turned down the liver. Looking back, I believe a combination of factors led to his decisions to turn down the opportunities. First, he was asymptomatic. Second, the chemoembolization had worked, completely dissolving the masses, so the procedure had been completely successful. Third, I truly think the thought of undergoing the procedure scared him to death. Fourth, he wanted to continue to use heroin. He prioritized his addiction over his own life. Sadly, in the summer of 2018, Pat was diagnosed with a thrombus—a cancerous mass—in his portal vein. The prognosis for the mass, especially because of its location, was poor, thereby excluding him from the liver transplant list.

This news was beyond devastating for my mother and Pat. Despite the diagnosis, Pat continued to forge ahead and participated in proton therapy; a targeted type of radiation that focuses on killing the cancer cells while salvaging the healthy liver tissue. This treatment was physically and emotionally draining for both my mom and Pat, so much so that Pat's physical condition got significantly worse. In turn, my mother's mental health spiraled out of control. Ultimately, my mom and Pat reverted to poor coping strategies and relapsed with a vengeance. After several months of proton therapy, Pat's condition did not improve. Upon learning about this prognosis, Pat was on a death mission, and my mother was along for the ride.

They began to use heroin, and in the Philadelphia area, what is mostly available is fentanyl. In an attempt to help them, I encouraged my mother to go to inpatient rehab and suggested that Pat participate in in-home hospice. I thought that if he had a death wish and wanted to kill himself, signing up for hospice and having access to legal opioids would help relieve his pain. This would be better than continuing to abuse fentanyl and dying of an illegal overdose. I also didn't want my mother to die alongside him. I knew that Pat would not beat the cancer and that he would die. However, I didn't want my mom to die before her time. I understood that my mother's depression and sadness overwhelmed her; however, I didn't want to see her die of an overdose. As difficult as it would be for me to say this out loud, a part of me did want my mother to die—not because I was mad or angry at her for relapsing nor because I felt that her actions were selfish, even though I understand that's par for the course with this disease. It was because I didn't want to see her suffer anymore. I almost prayed for a peaceful death for her, and in my mind, that death consisted of a fentanyl overdose.

Looking back, hospice was the worst idea. Rather than taking the medications to ease his physical pain and looking at it as an opportunity to spend quality time with his family, Pat went off the deep end, and so did my mother. They began to use fentanyl regularly in conjunction with the benzodiazepines and morphine that was being provided by hospice. Pat suffered from a drug-induced psychotic state for nearly four weeks. His sister Katherine intervened and helped to get him into a respite facility so that we could get my mother into the hospital. At this time, they were both injecting fentanyl, and my mother had an infected abscess on her right forearm. It was so bad that I worried that she would get sepsis or, even worse, endocarditis. Endocarditis is an infection of the lining of the heart chambers or valves. A blood infection or endocarditis would certainly kill her; she was sixty-six years old.

So, Katherine got her to the emergency room. At the same time, she worked to get Pat into a respite facility so that we could figure out what to do about his psychotic state. The doctors explained to us that if his ammonia levels elevated, he could become confused or even psychotic. So, I thought that elevated ammonia levels might be responsible for some of the behaviors that he was exhibiting. However, I also think the number of opioids he was doing largely contributed to his psychological presentation.

My mother stayed in the hospital for four days for the abscess, or cellulitis. Pat then remained on home hospice until we could get him into respite care. The respite care facility he was at was horrific. It was dirty, he was not appropriately monitored, and the care was poor. Further, because the appropriate medical benefit papers were not initiated by the facility or hospice, he would be kicked out after the respite. Fearful that going home would be a death sentence for both him and my mother because they would go back to using drugs right away, I ended up taking Pat to the hospital to get his mental and physical status reassessed. I hoped that once the emergency room physicians observed his mental state, that they would admit him to stabilize him. The plan worked, thank God.

Pat stayed in the hospital for the entire month of December. During this time, he attempted to abscond from the hospital. He reported having visual hallucinations, such as seeing rats on the floor and termites in the bathroom. He was not oriented to time or even place, and he would often make no sense when he spoke. Pat was always on point and very sharp. So seeing him in this state was devastating for everyone.

He was on a one-to-one, meaning that medical technicians stayed with him twenty-four hours a day to ensure that he did not attempt to leave the hospital. During this time, we initiated the appropriate paperwork to place him in a skilled nursing facility. We did so because if we put him and my mom together, they would continue to abuse heroin.

After my mother was discharged from the hospital, my sister and I were desperate to get her help.

My sister had lost her father in August 2017 to a fentanyl overdose. When all of these issues arose with Pat, and she saw that he and my mom had relapsed, she was furious initially. However, as the heaviness of the situation began to set in, her fury turned to severe sadness and fear that she would also lose our mother to a drug overdose.

At the time, my sister worked as a medical assistant at an addiction clinic that specialized in providing medication-assisted treatment

(MAT) to individuals who struggled with alcohol and opioid dependence. The doctor she worked for had a practice dedicated to helping individuals who struggled with substance use disorders. So, she reached out to the doctor and asked if he could help my mother. He agreed.

Unbeknownst to me, my sister shared my mom's situation with the doctor. She called me and asked if I could bring our mom into the office to meet with the doctor. With no hesitation or judgment, the doctor assessed my mother and placed her on buprenorphine.

For me, it was truly amazing to go through the process as both a professional and a daughter of someone who was suffering from opioid addiction. It was fascinating to watch them start her on buprenorphine. The doctor followed the induction process appropriately, and I got to watch the medication work and to observe her improving.

It was inspiring to see my sister jump into action to help our mom. She hadn't been very empathetic toward my mother and her addiction. Losing her father had been extremely hard for her. Over the years, my sister would get closer to our mom whenever she was doing well. But when our mother would relapse, my sister would intentionally separate herself. She would always express to me how angry she was at our mother, and she made it a point to not get too close to her because she always felt let down when she relapsed.

This time around was different. Although my sister was still mad at our mom, she was really afraid that she would lose yet another parent to a heroin overdose. Although seeing my sister reach out to help my mom was inspiring, it was also sad because, at the end of the day, she was a twenty-three-year-old kid. This twenty-three-year-old kid had had to take her father off life support due to a fentanyl overdose and, quite frankly, may have had to do the same for her mother at some point. Though I don't wish that on me or my sister, it is the reality. This disease does not care about human casualties and the sacrifices that others have to make.

Pat went into a skilled nursing facility, and the man who was once built like a linebacker became thin and frail.

Sadly, in the early morning hours of March 13th, 2019, Pat passed away in the hospice unit of the Holy Redeemer Hospital. His sister Katherine was curled up in a chair next to him. She played Pink Floyd for him and gently whispered to him that it was OK for him to let go. My mother, distraught over Pat's impending demise, could no longer bear to be at the hospital.

I was asleep in my bed with my four-year-old daughter dozing beside me when my bedroom door creaked open. My mother entered and stood at the foot of my bed, shaking as tears streamed down her face. She whispered so as not to wake my daughter, "Pat's gone."

With that, I quietly got out of bed, trying unsuccessfully to swallow my tears. I did not want my mother to completely break down, so I stopped crying, threw on a pair of yoga pants and a sweatshirt, and drove to Holy Redeemer, which was also where my children had been born. In an odd way, I was happy that Pat passed at Holy Redeemer, because it was a place that had brought me so much joy . . . a place where I had witnessed the birth of the most incredible people in my life: my son, Gregory, and my daughter, Natalee. Driving to the same hospital to say goodbye to Pat, who had made such a lasting impression on my children and me, was comforting.

For Pat's memorial service, we filled a life-sized picture frame with a collage of photos of Pat and placed it on an easel at the cemetery. Friends and family got up and shared their fondest memories. Even Chief of Adult Probation, Mike Gordon, showed up to say his goodbyes. What resonated with me most, however, was the sadness and grief that I saw in my seven-year-old son. From the time my son Gregory was born, he and Pat had had a special bond. Pat truly loved my son. Even now, my son talks about how much he misses his grandfather and how he wishes that Poppop could visit us from heaven.

All of this demonstrated further to me that even though people, like Pat, may have problems with substance abuse, they are in most other ways just like the rest of us, with dreams and hopes and people who will miss them when they are gone.

CHAPTER SIX

FINDING MY PURPOSE

Putting My Past to Good Use

As time-consuming as writing this book has been, it has been equally cathartic. Being able to connect all of the dots of my past and draw the lines between my upbringing and choice of profession, I am left in awe.

It's almost as if my purpose as a clinician in the field of addiction has been vastly influenced by my life experiences. You may be thinking, Why the heck would she want to work with this population of people when she was hurt in many ways by her own parents as they struggled with drug and alcohol abuse and mental health issues?

For me, the answer is simple. I believe I have been guided down this path, that the bruises and pain I endured have given me a thick skin, a protective armor I need to be an influential voice in this field. Unlike many authors who have written books on the topic of addiction, I feel as though I offer a unique perspective because I understand the struggle and pain caused by this disease through not only a professional, clinical, or intellectual lens; but a personal one as well.

Upon entering the doctoral program, my goal was to open a private therapy practice. I also believed that attending a clinical psychology program would give me the opportunity to "heal thyself." I believed that the knowledge I gained about mental illness and addiction would afford me the opportunity to understand the choices my parents did or did not make when it came to caring for themselves and caring for me. This is just what happened.

My professional knowledge helped me develop a stronger sense of empathy for my parents and aided me in my struggle to give myself permission to feel hurt and angry at them over the collateral damage. I have always put their feelings and needs before my own, and today, I find myself feeling compelled to protect them from the psychological pain that they caused me. I truly believe that they could not handle knowing that they hurt me. Because as dysfunctional or unconventional as their love for me may have been, I know that they loved me to the best of their ability.

While in the doctoral program, I had to complete clinical rotations to satisfy my degree requirements. All of the clinical rotations I selected focused on disenfranchised populations: individuals the general population looks down on. Those populations consisted of sex offenders, people struggling with drug addiction, violent offenders, and severely mentally ill individuals who had committed heinous crimes. Back then, I did not realize just how my choices to work with these individuals reflected my desire to gain a clearer understanding of and respect for my parents and those close to me who have struggled with trauma, depression, physical abuse, and addiction. The work I have done as a psychologist has been my way of trying to help my mother and understand my late father.

As much as I can be a resource for my mother to finally get the quality of help that she needs, she does not take advantage of it. Therefore, in helping individuals who want to be helped, I feel as though I am inadvertently helping my parents. The abuse that my parents endured as children and the abuse that they continued to place upon themselves as adults speaks to the lack of support and love that they were not privy to throughout their lives. Doing the work that I do, as a medical educator about addiction, to help individuals struggling with addiction and other severe mental illness makes me feel as though I am paying it forward, for my parents, in an indirect way.

For me, life became about my new family and my studies. I completed a master's degree in clinical and counseling psychology in the summer of 2011 and was accepted into the doctoral program, at Chestnut Hill College, for clinical psychology shortly thereafter.

Court Work

In 2016, I officially completed my doctoral program and began to look for post-doctoral fellowship opportunities. I worked part-time in a community mental health clinic, conducting group therapy for individuals who suffered from both drug addiction and severe mental illness. I also conducted individual psychotherapy sessions that consisted of a collaboration of motivational interviewing, family-systems, and a psychodynamic therapy approach. I enjoyed this work as I felt that it kept my finger on the pulse of individuals suffering from addiction.

I wrote my doctoral dissertation on how probation officers perceive individuals (probationers) on their caseloads with severe mental illness and or addiction. Through my research, I continued to develop a good relationship with Mike Gordon, Chief of Adult Probation in Montgomery County, PA, and Pasquale's childhood friend. He even attended my dissertation defense. After completing my educational requirements, the behavioral health provider that the Montgomery County Probation Department used for psychological evaluations for the Courts reached out to me to retain my services as a psychological evaluator. With this contract, I was tasked with going to the county correctional facility and assessing offenders prior to their release from prison in an effort to assist the Court in appropriately recommending mental health treatment for these individuals. I also worked closely with specialty Court programs such as Drug Court and Behavioral Health Court to assist judges, the probation department, and public defenders on determining offenders' required level of mental health care post-release from prison.

I truly loved this work for many reasons, but people would ask me if I was afraid for my safety, going into the prisons and spending time alone with offenders. My answer was always the same, "Not at all. I feel at home." Most folks who did not know my backstory chuckled, but the truth is, I felt very comfortable with the majority of the people I saw within the prison system. I would like to believe that my comfort level is due to the cast of characters who have played major roles in my life, from my parents to friends such as Jimmy-Joe.

The work was also very rewarding. Granted, a significant number of the people I saw would often re-offend, violating the terms of their probation for providing a "dirty urine" to the probation department. (A "dirty urine" occurs when a probationer uses an illicit substance, is drug-tested by the probation department, and produces a positive urine screen for an illicit substance(i.e., heroin, cocaine, LSD, PCP, etc.)).The first several minutes of meeting an inmate were often the tensest moments, as they did not know who I was or why I was there. After giving them my spiel and talking with them in a respectful manner, I could begin to see the tension dissipate.

There were certainly challenges: I am a Caucasian female, often dressed in business attire with a laptop opened in front of me, and I do not appear as though I can relate. Individuals looked at me and seemed to think: this doc doesn't know shit, and I am not telling her a damned thing about me and my life. But I tended to surprise people like this with how relatable I am.

Of course, I did not disclose my entire life story to my patients, but how I choose to approach them and talk with them tipped them off that I knew what's up. For example, if evaluating someone with significant drug issues, I asked them where they "copped" their drugs. They would often tell me they copped in Kensington, and I then disclosed that my family owned a bar in the area and that I'm familiar with Kenzo. This was my way of letting them know that they could not pull one over on me; I'm not as naive as I look!

My Medical Science Liaison Work

During the summer of 2017, I was looking for an opportunity within the pharmaceutical industry that would allow me to put my doctoral degree to use. A friend told me about Medical Science Liaisons (MSLs), doctoral-level professionals hired by pharmaceutical companies to educate medical doctors on the drugs they develop. For six months, I researched various drugs, pharmaceutical companies, and recruiting agencies. In talking with other MSLs in the field and recruiters, I learned that the majority of MSL positions are offered to folks with previous MSL experience. Well, I had none, but I did not let that deter me. I wanted to use my doctoral degree in a therapeutic area where I had experience and a vested interest. For me, it was addiction.

One day while surfing a job board for an MSL role, I came across a job that required experience and knowledge about the "disease of addiction." I immediately lit up and applied online. I wanted to create the best possible opportunity for an interview, so I searched for the chief medical officer (CMO) online and reached out to him directly. To my surprise, he returned my e-mail and we agreed to meet in person at a local Starbucks. I figured I would meet with him but had very low expectations because of my lack of experience in this specialty. Also, MSLs are typically medical doctors or pharmacists. As a clinical psychologist, I was not sure that I would have a shot. I decided to go for it anyway. The conversation I had with the CMO was about opioid use disorder, and individuals who are dependent on opioids.

During our meeting, I had the same feeling of comfort that I experienced assessing inmates at the prison. I felt at home. What are the odds that I would have the opportunity to work in the field of addiction, especially Opioid Use Disorder, educating healthcare providers on the disease of addiction? Good, as it turns out: I was hired.

The knowledge I have gained through bearing witness to my parents' addiction and the understanding I have achieved from a neurobiological and psychological aspect about drug addiction and mental illness are immeasurable. Fortunately, I can now share this knowledge with other clinicians who are also interested in working with individuals struggling with substance use disorders.

In the rooms at NA/AA meetings, people will often refer to God or another higher power giving them the strength they need to continue to live a clean and sober lifestyle.

I credit my journey to both to a higher power and to my parents because, despite their struggles, they have been instrumental in helping me gain a more profound understanding of the disease of addiction. Their experience and the experiences of others in this book have given me a genuine empathy for those suffering with this disease.

ADDICTION EDUCATION HANDBOOK

Conceptualizing drug addiction as a neurobiological, midbrain disease offers psychological protection for people who are struggling with addiction, not to mention for their family members, spouses/partners, and friends.

For instance, for a long time, I believed that my mother consciously chose to use drugs (heroin, alcohol, benzodiazepines) rather than care for my sister and me. I felt resentful toward her. There were times when I was riddled with sadness; I just wanted her to stop using drugs and be the mom I had idealized in my head, the mom who would take care of me, rather than me taking care of her.

The more I pursued my education and learned about this disease, the more I realized my mother's compulsion to use drugs was directly correlated to chronic relapsing, which is a midbrain disease. Her capability to put her responsibility for me and my sister before her desire to get high was over-ridden by the disease. Learning about the neurobiology of addiction from leaders in the field, such as Dr. Nora Volkow, afforded me the opportunity to become truly empathetic, rather than angry, with my mom.

Don't get me wrong: the situations she put me in and the feelings of anger, sadness, and even fear she evoked in me were very real. However, learning that her poor decisions and selfish behaviors were a symptom of this disease helped me develop a psychologically protective armor when I needed to emotionally interact with her. I realize it seems sad that I needed to emotionally safeguard my feelings for my mother to protect my own heart. Yet had I not gained a firm understanding of this disease, I would still be trying to "fix" her "deficiencies of character" when in reality, she has a chronic, psychiatric illness. Her damaged brain has broken many hearts, but understanding that this was not her conscious intent is vital in helping her and, just as importantly, in healing me.

Knowledge of the disease of addiction also provides a psychological layer of protection to those suffering from addiction. When they are actively engaged in their addiction, these individuals often pursue behaviors that are detrimental to themselves and their loved ones, leading to feelings of remorse and self-loathing. Comprehending that their addiction is an actual disease and that the poor decisions they make related to interpersonal relationships and their own physical and emotional safety have been influenced by this disease gives them the opportunity to forgive themselves. We all need forgiveness, and this must start with forgiving ourselves.

All too often, of course, people who try to "get clean" will relapse. Although relapse is an inescapable phase of the disease of addiction, these repeated, unsuccessful attempts at a sober lifestyle may contribute to overwhelming feelings of guilt and shame that are associated with the behaviors they engaged in when they were "using."

Also, some may perceive their relapse as failures and internalize that relapse as signifying that they're not worthy of recovery. Negative self-talk during the recovery process can present a huge barrier to sticking with the recovery process. They may think, "I'm a loser. I have hurt so many people, and I have done so much damage to my life that I am not worthy of a second chance." Or they may say, "I am too afraid to get clean because of the overwhelming feelings such as guilt and shame I will feel if I stop using drugs."

These painful feelings, along with the neurobiological impact that this disease has on the brain, contributes to relapse. Furthermore, people struggling with this disease often lack healthy coping strategies; poor coping strategies, coupled with a genetic or biological disposition for addiction, and stressful situations, increased these individuals' vulnerability to drug addiction in the first place.

Defining Addiction

Addiction is not a lifestyle that any of us would want to adopt. I doubt anyone wakes up one morning and lists "become a drug addict" as a life goal. However, remember that addiction is a disease state, similar to diabetes or asthma. People who eventually make the transition from recreationally using drugs to becoming dependent on them demonstrate that their ability to choose has been overridden by their compulsion to use drugs. A complete lack of self-control and poor decision making are the hallmarks of addiction.

A person who doesn't suffer from addiction may feel that labeling addiction as a disease is simply an excuse, a way of enabling "junkies" to continue to get high as they blaze a trail of destruction and chaos. And as I've said, prior to pursuing my doctorate in clinical psychology, along with educating myself on this disease and talking with my parents about their drug abuse struggles, I felt the same way. Finally, rather than continuing to marinate in feelings of anger and resentment toward my mom for being placed in multiple situations where I suffered from the consequences of her drug addiction, I decided to learn. From my perspective, attaining knowledge about my mother's addiction equated to peace of mind. As the child of someone who suffers from this disease, I didn't want to believe that my mother did not love me enough to stop using drugs. Instead, I found comfort in learning that her drug addiction had morphed my mom into someone who was self-involved and more in love with getting high than loving and caring for me.

Knowledge has helped me conceptualize my parents' struggles and challenges as being directly related to their drug addiction(s) and mental health issues. The knowledge I have gained has also enabled me to feel empathy for my parents and others who are like them. Although empathy does not replace the feelings of anger and sadness, it has allowed me to forgive and release the anger I once felt toward my parents, a resentment that sprang from feelings of being deprived of my childhood and healthy interactions with my parents.

Oddly enough, I did not blame myself. I clearly understood that it was their demons keeping them from being the ideal parents. My parents' transparency about their struggles allowed me to gain insight, even as a child, into their issues, and the verbal and physical affection they displayed made me feel loved. In other words, my parents loved me to the best of their ability. In turn, the manner in which I perceived my parents and myself, even as a child, reflects how they interacted with me despite their transgressions as individuals struggling with addiction and psychological dysfunction.

Twenty-five Years of Treatment: Successes and Failures

Although I am aware that I idealize my father, I know that my mother has consistently reached out for drug and alcohol and mental health treatment over the years. In contrast, my father adopted a more "cold turkey" approach to getting clean—abruptly stopping on his own without any medication-assisted treatment or psychotherapy to address his prevailing psychological traumas.

My mother became addicted to prescription pain medication after suffering from tooth pain in her early 40s. Yet it's important to emphasize that prior to becoming addicted to prescription pain medication (i.e., Percocet, Vicodin, etc.), she had struggled with alcohol abuse.

Sharing this information and using my mother as an example brings to life the most current theory of addiction: it is a brain disease caused by genetic and environmental factors. My mother was genetically predisposed to addiction and mental health issues. (My grandmother abused alcohol and then Darvocet after it was initially prescribed to her for chronic back pain, and my grandfather struggled with alcoholism).

Furthermore, like her parents, my mother drank alcohol in an attempt to elevate her mood and decrease her feelings of overwhelming anxiety. This ultimately led to abuse as the effects of alcohol and other substances last for a limited time. Decreased inhibitions and a feeling of euphoria take place when an individual is intoxicated because neurotransmitters in the brain, such as dopamine and serotonin, are substantially increased.

Consistent drug use causes an intense, abundant release of these neurotransmitters which results in a euphoric state. When the effects of the drugs and alcohol wear off, however, the individuals' moods plummet even lower than before taking the drugs or alcohol. The beginning stages of drug and alcohol use are initiated in an effort to attain that feeling of a powerful euphoria. As drug use persists, though, the euphoria becomes less intense as the body's tolerance increases. However, persistence in trying to attain euphoria transitions into dependence because, as the ecstasy dissipates, their moods become significantly more dysphoric. In other words, even though euphoria is no longer achieved with persistent drug and alcohol use because of tolerance, it continues because individuals become physically and psychologically dependent on those feelings.

In talking with my mother and many others who have struggled with drug and alcohol use, the words I would often hear are, "I have to use to function and feel somewhat 'normal.' Because if I don't use, I won't be able to get out of bed."

As patients have related the cyclical aspects of persistent drug use to me, I have better understood the gradation of my mother's drug use. For instance, my mother started by abusing opioid pain medication. When her prescription ran out because of misuse/abuse, she turned to "copping" or buying opioid pain medication on the street. However, procuring pain medication in this manner is expensive. My mother's addiction to pain medication consumed so much of her life that she resorted to stealing, lying, and manipulating to get the money needed to support her drug use.

(Recall the earlier story about the day my mother and our friend, Jimmy-Joe, orchestrated robbing the hair salon where she worked!) In addition to making poor decisions and having to face their negative consequences, her choices, of course, also had a markedly negative impact on my sister and me.

After several years of abusing pain medication, my mother was turned on to heroin. (The first time she used was with Jimmy-Joe.) Like many people who become addicted to heroin, she never thought she would fall victim to this "type" of drug abuse.

You see, within the community of individuals who abuse opioids, intravenous heroin addicts are considered the "lowest of the low." People who abuse prescribed pain medications often do not see themselves as "drug addicts" because they were prescribed these opioid medications. In contrast, people who abuse heroin are using an illicit substance, a street drug.

Initially, my mother used heroin intranasally (snorted it). She had moved from abusing opioid pain medication to heroin, which was cost-effective at first. Initially, she used one or two bags of heroin a day. As her use progressed and her tolerance to the drug grew, the number of bags she used increased, and of course, the cost increased.

The method of administration is also factored into the intensity of the "high" and the related cost of the habit. For example, after my mother built a tolerance to using heroin intranasally, she began to "skin-pop." Skin-popping is a slang term to describe an intramuscular injection. With this method, people will inject themselves with a syringe where there is dense tissue or fatty areas, most commonly in the arms and legs. Initially, this method may give the individual a more intense or "better" high compared with snorting or intranasal use.

However, the problem is that then, users continue to up the ante in search of a better high. My mother eventually began to use heroin intravenously, and when she made this transition, her addiction grew much more insidious, and the cost of her habit soared. Electronics, jewelry, or anything of any monetary value, including her wedding ring, were pawned to support her addiction. My mother called family members and concocted tales of want and woe, using my younger sister or me as an excuse for needing cash. When I began waitressing, she stole the tips I made (and soon, just about anything else of monetary value I had).

After nearly a year of heroin abuse and several years of opioid pain medication abuse and dependency, my mother grew physically, emotionally, and psychologically exhausted and finally asked for help. At first, she participated in a "medically monitored detox," which usually lasts five to six days in an inpatient rehabilitation facility or hospital. Methadone, a full opioid agonist (a substance that imitates a physiological response when combined with a receptor), is used in liquid form to assist individuals with withdrawal from heroin and pain medication. Those who participate in a medical detox are titrated (the balance of the drug is adjusted) completely from heroin and opioid pain medication by using decreasing doses of methadone.

What Happens in Rehab

More recently, there has been a push toward having inpatient facilities initiate and maintain individuals on medication-assisted treatment in an effort to decrease their risk of relapse and potential overdose upon discharge from inpatient care.

On day one of a medical detox, a patient may receive 70 mg of methadone; each subsequent day, the dose is lowered. By day six of a medically monitored detox, patients are given their last dose of methadone, which is typically around 5 mg.

Further, buprenorphine, a partial opioid agonist, is also used to detox individuals over that six-day window. The physical withdrawal symptoms of severe opioid use disorder are commonly described as the worst flu-like symptoms one can experience. Gastrointestinal cramping, nausea, abdominal pain, diarrhea, body aches, restless leg, chills, irritability, anxiety (panic), insomnia, anhedonia, low mood (depression), watering eyes, running nose, and headache are common symptoms of patients suffering through an opioid withdrawal. A medical detox helps protect individuals from the physical symptoms associated with heroin and pain medication withdrawal.

After completing a medically monitored detox, participation in inpatient rehabilitation is often recommended. For most people, insurance companies may cover the six-day medical detox, which is accompanied by a twenty-one- to twenty-eight-day stay in an inpatient rehabilitation facility. The quality of treatment that an individual receives is often based upon their insurance coverage. In some cases, family members may offer to pay for a patient's rehabilitation, but in both my personal and professional experiences, most individuals struggling with drug addiction often require multiple stays in an inpatient rehabilitation facility and/or participation in a medically monitored detox before they can sustain longer term sobriety. It is glaringly obvious that if a person does not have some form of insurance coverage (i.e., commercial or Medicaid), it becomes difficult to provide treatment.

Typically, after a patient successfully completes a stint in an inpatient rehabilitation facility, they are provided with the option to return home or participate in a step-down program that may require residing in a therapeutic community or a sober living house.

For many people struggling with this disease, returning home is not an option. Prior to seeking treatment, patients may have been asked to leave their homes because of their unhealthy behaviors. They may also be in the midst of a separation or divorce from their partners and may have been couch surfing. In other circumstances, they may have been living with other individuals who were addicted, making a return to that house unsafe for their continued recovery. In some circumstances, individuals may have been living on the streets because of the severity of their addiction.

A step-down program is commonly recommended for most people who have successfully completed their inpatient rehabilitation. A step-down program is a therapeutic community where individuals live while learning how to reintegrate as productive members of society. Around-the-clock clinical staff are present at the facility. Residents participate in mental health treatment that often consists of psychiatric care (i.e., psychotropic medications) to manage psychological disorders such as depression or anxiety. They also participate in weekly individual psychotherapy so that they can begin to learn healthy coping mechanisms rather than turning to illicit drug use when they feel stressed or overwhelmed.

Residents may also participate in group therapy, which focuses on drug and alcohol counseling and other mental health issues such as depression, bipolar I/II, and so forth. While engaging in treatment at a therapeutic community, participants also receive case management services so that they can begin to find employment and a place to live before being released from the therapeutic community. An individual resides in a therapeutic community between six and twelve months before being discharged into independent living.

Aside from the option of residing in a therapeutic community that affords individuals structure (i.e., random urine screens, curfew, Narcotics Anonymous [NA] meetings), mental health services, case management services, and accountability for their actions/plans, sober living houses are also an option that some individuals choose upon being released from an inpatient rehabilitation facility.

Unlike a therapeutic community, a sober living house is often managed by an individual who is recovering from drug and/or alcohol addiction. The house typically accommodates under a dozen same-gender individuals. Participants pay rent weekly to reside in the house and are encouraged to live an abstinence-based lifestyle. Often, in this environment, residents are encouraged to attend NA and/or Alcoholics Anonymous (AA) meetings on a daily basis. Mental health services and case management services are not offered in sober living homes, but treatment is encouraged.

The difference here is that these individuals do not have the same level of structure offered in a therapeutic community setting. Curfew and urine screens may be administered in a sober living setting, but each house tends to institute its own rules, which are based heavily on the house owners and live-in house managers. Sadly, in some instances, these houses are run poorly because the house managers themselves may relapse and continue to use until the house owner is made aware of the situation.

In many cases, the owners of these sober living houses may have a dozen or so homes that they own because this is an extremely lucrative business model. In turn, they are not always on-site at every house, and in these circumstances, people often find that the rate of relapse is high if the house manager is newer in his or her recovery or if the house manager does not continue to work on his or her "own recovery." Further, both therapeutic communities and sober living houses are residential programs that typically last up to twelve months before residents successfully complete the program or leave of their own volition.

Individuals who complete an inpatient rehabilitation program (i.e., roughly twenty-eight to thirty days) and who may have a stable environment to return to upon their discharge may participate in an intensive-outpatient program (IOP), which typically includes a minimum of a combination of group and individual therapy every week.

In an IOP, individuals typically spend several hours at a time, several times per week at a mental health clinic participating in a psychoeducation-based drug and alcohol didactic group, process group therapy, and individual psychotherapy with a licensed professional counselor, certified addiction counselor, or psychologist. The quality of mental health treatment that individuals receive in an intensive-outpatient setting is similar to the quality of care received in an inpatient setting because it is based on insurance coverage and/or the ability to pay for services. Keep in mind, that those diagnosed and identified with opioid use disorder generally do not have the best insurance coverage or the ability to afford quality care (unless they are under twenty-six years old and on their parents' insurance plan or are on their spouse's insurance plan). This does not mean that all clinicians and facilities that take Medicaid or county-funded insurance are "bad." It only means that the quality and frequency of care are often inconsistent.

Co-Occurring Mental Illness with Substance Use Disorders

It is quite common that patients who use drugs have also been diagnosed with other substance abuse issues and accompanying psychological disorders, such as major depressive disorder (MDD), generalized anxiety disorder (GAD), post-traumatic stress disorder (PTSD), bipolar I and II disorders, attention-deficit hyperactivity disorder (ADHD), a thought disorder such as schizophrenia, or even an undiagnosed learning disorder.

For instance, many adolescents who have never received educational support, yet have needed help addressing a learning disorder, often act out in an effort to deflect attention from their academic challenges. Often, these adolescents may be inaccurately labeled with ADHD or even oppositional defiant disorder (ODD) because their behaviors meet the diagnostic criteria for these diagnoses; however, a closer look often finds that their behaviors are actually symptomatic of an underlying learning deficit.

For example, as a young child, my mother began to suffer from anxiety. Her parents constantly argued because my grandfather was a heavy drinker who had a hard time keeping away from other women. At times, the arguments became physical. Out of her three sisters, my mother was always the one who tried to stop the fighting; she was also the one tasked with going down to the bar and convincing my grandfather to come home. Keep in mind, my grandmother suffered from bipolar I disorder, which is mood instability marked by severe fluctuations in mood from depression to mania. When she was manic, she would often bring strangers into her home and drink and party with them for days. Like my grandmother, my mother was "blessed" with severe anxiety that turned into panic attacks, and as her anxiety grew more debilitating, she began to feel depressed. Into her late teens and early 20s, she began to experience panic attacks. Similar to the generational pattern observed in my mommom's and grandfather's relationship, my mother selected a partner— my father— who had a history of being both unfaithful and addicted to heroin and methamphetamines.

After giving birth to me at the age of twenty-seven, my mother suffered from severe postpartum depression, which was accompanied by anxiety. At this point, she began to drink and use Valium, a benzodiazepine, to calm her nerves. As her mental health—bombarded with external factors such as my father's infidelity and his own struggle with addiction—grew more unbalanced, so did my mother's urge to "self-medicate" by using illicit substances to numb out the psychological pain. In the process of using drugs and alcohol to make her feel better, another monster known as addiction soon reared its ugly head, complicating matters even more.

Medication-Assisted Treatment

There are multiple forms of medication-assisted treatments available for individuals with opioid use disorder. For over four decades, methadone, a long-acting agonist at the mu-Opioid receptors that run throughout the central nervous system, has been dispensed in an oral liquid form known as Dolophine. This treatment is generally given at opioid treatment programs or methadone clinics. Methadone's pharmacodynamic properties are similar to illicit opioids such as heroin, in that the more you use, the "higher" you get, hence why it is a full opioid agonist. However, methadone maintenance programs for individuals who are dependent on opioids require daily visits to a methadone clinic so that they can receive a dose to manage opioid withdrawal symptoms without getting "high." These clinics are governed by a variety of federal regulations that describe how and when methadone can be dispensed. Participation in methadone maintenance programs will typically carry a minimal expense to patients because these programs are largely funded by the government.

Buprenorphine/naloxone combination drug products such as Zubsolv (sublingual tablet), Suboxone (transmucosal film), and Bunavail (transmucosal film) are taken orally, either under the tongue (sublingually) or buccally (in the cheek). There are also generic buprenorphine or naloxone medications available in both tablet and film formulations. These products contain buprenorphine, a partial opioid agonist that binds to the mu-Opioid receptors, protecting individuals from painful withdrawal symptoms while decreasing their desire to "get high." Buprenorphine has what is called a "ceiling effect," meaning that individuals who are addicted to opioids cannot "get high" on buprenorphine if they take more of it. Buprenorphine plays two major roles: (1) it prevents debilitating physical withdrawal symptoms, and (2) it manages cravings. With these formulations, naloxone, an opioid antagonist, is added to deter individuals from trying to misuse these medications by injecting them.

Buprenorphine-monotherapy or Subutex, the brand name, is a sublingual tablet that only contains buprenorphine without the naloxone.

Without naloxone, individuals may experience an easier time trying to inject this medication because it does not contain naloxone and will not precipitate withdrawal. Keep in mind that naloxone is fused into buprenorphine and naloxone combination products, such as those mentioned above, to deter parenteral abuse. There is also a buprenorphine subcutaneous monthly injection available on the market called Sublocade. Individuals must be stabilized on sublingual buprenorphine for seven days prior to being transferred to the monthly injection. Another medication called Probuphine is an implant that contains buprenorphine and is indicated for those who have achieved and sustained prolonged clinical stability on low-to-moderate doses (i.e., no more than 8 mg per day) of sublingual buprenorphine daily.

In higher doses, naloxone is also used as a reversal agent for individuals who have overdosed on opioids. Narcan is a branded naloxone product that is administered intranasally to individuals who have overdosed on opioids.

Naltrexone is a full opioid antagonist. To picture how naltrexone works, think of a two-ton elephant sitting on top of the receptor, blocking the effects of heroin, alcohol, and other opioids. Naltrexone comes in both tablet form and in an injectable form known as Vivitrol, which is administered monthly and is indicated for the treatment of alcohol use disorder and opioid use disorder. Because naltrexone is nonaddictive, it has been more widely accepted within the abstinence-based treatment approach. The criminal justice system (i.e., drug court programs) also tends to prefer that individuals be treated with naltrexone rather than buprenorphine or methadone. However, I believe that more recently, the criminal justice system is taking the appropriate steps to learn about all forms of medication-assisted treatment in an effort to more effectively manage offenders with opioid use disorders and other substance use disorders.

Nonetheless, treatment for opioid use disorder should be determined collaboratively by healthcare providers and the patient, not the criminal justice system. The patient's treatment team should consist of the healthcare provider, therapist, and, to a degree, the patients —their input and opinions should be considered. Every individual's care should be customized based on the information collected regarding their drug and alcohol history, medical history, psychiatric history, current living situation, legal situation, and any other factors that may influence their recovery.

According to the Federal Drug Administration (FDA), the duration or length of time an individual can be maintained on medication-assisted forms of treatment depends on each individual's situation and risk/benefit profile. On the one hand, someone like my mom, who severely abused opioids for over two decades, may be on medication-assisted treatment for the rest of her life, and this would be acceptable because the risk associated with discontinuing her medication-assisted treatment may result in an unintentional overdose or even death. On the other hand, some patients I have worked with have successfully titrated or been weaned off of medication-assisted treatment with the support and help of healthcare providers. The decision to do so was not impulsive, nor was it dictated by someone outside the healthcare system. . It was discussed at length and collaboratively decided upon by the patient, healthcare providers, and mental health professionals while ensuring the appropriate supports (i.e., increasing psychotherapy) were put in place for that individual.

The Rise of Fentanyl

Over the past several years, there has been a significant increase in synthetic opioid (such as fentanyl) overdoses among illicit drug users. Fentanyl remains the primary driver behind the ongoing opioid crisis, with it being involved in more deaths than any other illicit drug (Drug Threat Assessment, 2019). There have been multiple synthetic fentanyl analogs identified by the National Forensic

Laboratory Information System (NFLIS), such as carfentanil, a fatal fentanyl analog, as well as acetyl fentanyl, furanyl fentanyl, and others. According to the Center for Disease Control and Prevention (CDC), synthetic opioid-involved deaths increased by 47% from 2016 to 2017. Why is this important?

It is important because medications such as buprenorphine have pharmacodynamic properties that can protect individuals who have been intentionally or inadvertently exposed to fentanyl because of its long half-life (the amount of time required for half of a substance to disintegrate). Yes, I said inadvertent exposure to fentanyl. Many individuals who are now dependent on fentanyl did not seek it out.

These individuals may have been dependent on prescription opioids such as oxycodone or heroin and were exposed to fentanyl under the guise that they were buying another opioid. For those who are dependent on heroin, fentanyl comes in either a powder form, like the heroin seen mostly on the East Coast, or a "black tar" form, earning its name because of its stark resemblance to the tar used for roofs, on the West Coast. Fentanyl was initially mixed in or "laced" in heroin, and individuals were unaware that they were even being exposed to it. As far as pain medication or pills are concerned, purchasing them on the illicit drug market increases one's chance of receiving a counterfeit pill disguised as oxycodone. The pill is the same color and is even scored to look like a prescription pill, but in reality, it is fentanyl that is pressed to look like an Oxycontin or Percocet. Since the arrival of fentanyl into the illicit drug market, overdose deaths have continued to rise across the United States.

Places and Faces in Recovery

As a clinician who has worked closely with this patient population, I have learned that relapse is a part of recovery because addiction is a chronic, relapsing midbrain disease. Yet I have seen people recover and move on to live fulfilling lives, even though they may have a "lapse" in their recovery journey.

A lapse differs from a relapse, in that with a lapse, a person may use drugs or alcohol for a brief period; for example, they may use once or twice before getting back on "the wagon," working on their recovery again, surrounding themselves with sober places and faces, and abstaining from illicit substances.

Conversely, the individuals I have worked with who relapse often vanish from care for an extended period of time and continue to use heavily again. They often think, "The hell with it. I just used and lost all of my clean time. I've let down my friends, family, and those who hold me accountable (i.e., probation or healthcare providers). So, I am just going to keep riding this train and using because I'm a loser."

Individuals who are engaging in psychotherapy are provided with the psychological tools to decrease this negative self-talk and begin to view a lapse as a mistake rather than as a colossal failure. Recovery is a daily, lifelong commitment. It takes work to maintain sobriety. It's like being a parent; once you're a parent, you're always a parent, even when you're away from your kids on vacation. In recovery, there are no vacation days. Your number one priority is your recovery because if it does not come first, everything and everyone around you suffers.

After years of working with folks struggling with substance use disorders, I have learned the hard way that they are always a step—or twenty steps—ahead of healthcare providers. Those in active addiction often have above-average IQs and street-savvy. (My dad, who had no formal education, was one of the smartest individuals I knew, and he certainly developed street smarts from his experiences as a drug user.) People with minimal resources who have made the decision to use opioids will put these street smarts to work, often resorting to selling the same medications intended to help them stop abusing opioids.

For example, in the late 1990s, my mom was on methadone. She would wake up at 6:00 a.m. and drive thirty minutes to a methadone clinic; often, she would later sell her methadone so she could purchase heroin. Methadone is dispensed in liquid form. Rather than swallowing the Methadone when they handed it to her, my mother, given a chance, would spit the methadone out into a bottle she had brought with her and then sell it for cash. I know it sounds gross, ingesting methadone that was in someone else's mouth, but this kind of behavior is common. This same type of behavior also occurs with individuals who sell or trade their buprenorphine for illicit opioids. Keep in mind that again, these medications were developed to help people get off of illicit opioids and that maladaptive behaviors such as selling medication, lying, and manipulating are symptoms that individuals demonstrate when they are not actively working on their recovery.

When behaviors like this are observed, it's a clear indication that patients require a more structured approach to treatment. Hence, the statement I made earlier about medication-assisted treatment being just a piece of a large treatment pie is important here. Although medication-assisted treatment such as buprenorphine is excellent for managing opioid withdrawal symptoms and cravings, it is not "magic." For instance, taking medications will not fix the interpersonal issues created as a result of drug abuse; a more complete approach is required.

Healthcare providers must participate in additional mental health training to receive a special waiver known as a Drug Addiction Treatment Act (DATA) waiver, which permits them to prescribe buprenorphine. These healthcare providers are tasked with coordinating the appropriate mental health referrals and the collaboration of care with mental health professionals to ensure that their patients are also seeking treatment for the behavioral aspect of addiction. In addition to helping patients develop healthy, positive coping strategies to decrease their frequency of relapse, mental health services, such as psychotherapy, will help people address other psychiatric issues, such as feelings of depression, anxiety, and even trauma related to their drug use.

The negative toll that drug use takes on every aspect of a person's life can be heartbreaking. For instance, I worked with a young couple who had six children. The woman suffered from significant, untreated postpartum depression. Initially, she was prescribed opioid pain medication to manage the pain from her cesarean section. She eventually began to abuse the medication, claiming it helped her get through the day. With every delivery, she was prescribed more opioid pain medication. However, between each pregnancy, she was buying opioids off the street. Eventually, her use spiraled out of control when both she and her husband began to use heroin. Because they were unable to care for their children appropriately, the Department of Health and Human Services stepped in and placed the children in foster care. As a result of their drug abuse, the couple's marriage failed, they lost custody of their children, and the woman's depression grew so severe that she was placed in a psychiatric facility. So even though buprenorphine eventually helped the woman abstain from opioid abuse, she still required mental health treatment to address her depression, the loss of her children, and the collapse of her marriage.

In working with those who struggle with substance use disorders, I learned that it is imperative that they not only be evaluated and treated medically for these disorders, but that they also be helped psychologically. Taking medication for opioid use disorder without participating in psychotherapy can be like driving a car while blindfolded; a driver's license doesn't mean you can drive when you can't see. Medication gives you the license to drive, but the skills you learn and the insights you gain in psychotherapy become the vision you need to navigate the road ahead.

From a clinical perspective, the patients who tend to do the best in their recovery are those who are under the care of a physician who (1) understands the psychology behind the disease of addiction, (2) appropriately monitors their patients (i.e., random urine screens, collaborating with mental health professionals), and (3) truly expresses concern and provides treatment for their patients as opposed to viewing their practice as an opportunity for financial gain. For example, some healthcare providers charge patient's cash for monthly visits, which may range from $150 and up, to allow these patients to refill their buprenorphine prescription.

Many inpatient rehabilitation facilities and twelve-step fellowship programs such as AA and NA encourage abstinence, meaning that an individual would refrain from using the alcohol and illicit substances on which they have become both physically and psychologically dependent. However, when it comes to medications such as buprenorphine, developed to aid individuals in their physical recovery from opioid dependence, fellowship programs situated in the abstinence-based model approach perceive these forms of medication-assisted treatment as "replacing one opioid for another."

Gaining a clear understanding of the pharmacodynamic properties of these medications and how they work to calm a frazzled brain that has been severely overstimulated by persistent opioid abuse may be the kind of education needed for not only the dedicated members of twelve-step fellowship programs, but also for the public at large. In other words, some do not believe you are clean and whole-heartedly working on your recovery if you are taking buprenorphine (even if prescribed). This dissension within the recovery community reflects a rigid way of conceptualizing this disease. Recovery is a very personal and unique journey for every individual. What may have worked for one person (i.e., the abstinence-based model) may not work for another.

Treatment for individuals with this disease should be "individualized." A cookie-cutter approach does not apply well because everyone's journey is different.

FOR THOSE GROWING UP AROUND ADDICTION

n the rooms at NA/AA meetings, people will often refer to a higher power or God giving them the strength they need to continue to live a clean and sober lifestyle. My dad, although he did not subscribe to any formal, organized religion, believed in God.

I credit my journey to both the mantra repeated in the rooms about a higher power and to my parents because, despite their struggles, they have been instrumental in helping me gain a more profound understanding about the disease of addiction. Their experience and the experiences I have described here have given me a genuine empathy for those suffering from this disease.

However, as I near the end of this book, I have come to realize that I may have neglected to emphasize the effect it had on me, growing up in the kind of family I did. No one escapes unscathed from these types of situations; some do get out alive, but they do not get out without scars and some sort of psychological damage. How could they?

For me, I believe all the craziness I experienced growing up with parents who struggled with drug addiction and mental illness has, at the very least, left me a bit neurotic (just ask my husband!).

Further, I believe all of this led to my desire to prove myself to me and to the world, to be as perfect as I could be, which grew from the feelings of insecurity and embarrassment that I felt every day being part of my family. I presented myself in a way that I believed would not allow people to feel sorry for me; I wasn't going to be anyone's charity case. The fact is that I always felt judged by others because of my parents' lifestyle and poor behaviors. I did everything I could to disassociate myself from their image.

As is so often the case with perfectionism, the pressure I put on myself to not be judged by others for the parents I had was often overwhelming. I strove for perfection in everything I did—how I looked, how I acted, how I performed in school, and how I did at work. As much as striving for perfection in everything I did has paid off for me (becoming a doctor, having a successful career and a great family, etc.), the amount of pressure I put on myself can be debilitating at times. I struggle with anxiety, that is, excessive worry about things and events outside of my control. Although I worked hard to get where I am, I worry whether or not I deserve to be happy. I have a difficult time sitting back, reflecting, and simply enjoying life at times.

I believe it is one of the great burdens of the human race that we have a very difficult time balancing our desire to move forward and achieve with our ability to accept and embrace our lives and be happy. When this struggle becomes unhealthy, it is something known as the "hedonic treadmill," which is the contradiction stating that when people make more money or accomplishes more goals, their expectations rise in tandem with the goals they've achieved, resulting in never possessing the ability to gain permanent or long-lasting happiness. The term was first used by Brickman and Campbell, but it goes back to other writers, including the theologian and philosopher St. Augustine, who wrote, "A true saying it is, desire hath no rest; is infinite in itself, endless; and as one calls it, a perpetual rack or horsemill."

Yet despite all my own psychological issues, the fact remains that I have a great career, a great family, and a great life. The lesson therein, for anyone growing up in circumstances similar to mine, is that you can avoid the fate that tormented your family. You can excel and become as great as you want. You are your own person. You don't bear the sins of your father or mother or even their proclivities or tendencies. You deserve happiness. Look back to learn from the mistakes of others. Then look forward to what can be. And don't be afraid to take on the world and win.

Myths, like all things in constant use, break and are fixed again, become lost and are found, and the one who finds them and fixes them, the handyman who recycles them, is what Claude Lévi-Strauss calls a *bricoleur*—a term that he made famous even in English-speaking circles—and that the English used to call a "rag-and-bones man." Mythemes are made in what the poet William Butler Yeats (in "The Circus Animals") called "the foul rag and bone shop of the heart." In the ecology of narratives, recycling is a very old process. Each telling of a myth draws upon these rags and bones, and each piece has its own previous life-history that it brings into the story. . . . [Lévi-Strauss] is the one who taught us that every myth is driven by the obsessive need to solve a paradox *that cannot be solved*. His critics see him as reducing myths to logical oppositions, but I see him as illuminating human ambivalences. Paradoxes are to Lévi-Strauss what whales were to Captain Ahab.

—Wendy Doniger

Excerpted from the foreword by Wendy Doniger for *Myth and Meaning: Cracking the Code of Culture* by Claude Lévi-Strauss (Shocken, 1995). Reprinted by permission of the author.

PRAYER BEFORE PRAYER

MARK HAGE

He stood and hurried out and there was a scent of the earth: maidenhair, schist, disrupted loam.

He arrived where they met for quiet lunches, for their bread and olive oil.

She reported her disappointments. She ate fast. He matched her speed, the speed where food becomes volumetric and taste is halved.

At the edge of the window shade, he could see through a crack the high-rise beyond. He closed and angled an eye until the edges of the shade and the building, one soft and one dolomitic, aligned as one.

These were the distractions at his disposal. The usual restaurant table, its ornaments. Ordering the meats well-done.

Without looking up, she said she had forgotten to bring cash.

"They don't take credit cards," she said.

Maybe she should go get some money.

Wait. Wait for what?

She piled the bills decisively.

He knew of the small gaps before what comes next.

PAINTINGS AND SCULPTURES

LOUIS FRATINO

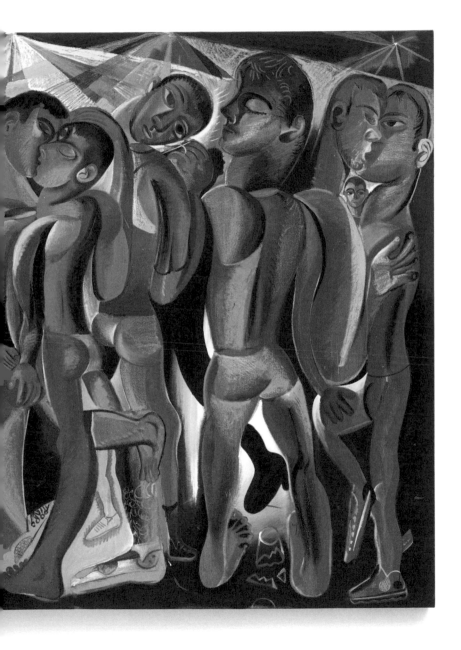

Page 124. *Kissing Couple*, 2019, oil on canvas, 75" × 60". Courtesy of the artist and Sikkema Jenkins & Co., New York.

Page 125. *Among Women Only*, 2020, oil on canvas, 80" × 65". Courtesy of the artist and Sikkema Jenkins & Co., New York.

Page 126. *Tom in Albisola*, 2020, oil on canvas, 14" × 11". Courtesy of the artist and Sikkema Jenkins & Co., New York.

Page 127. *I Keep My Treasure in My Ass*, 2019, oil on canvas, 85 ¾" × 65". Courtesy of the artist and Sikkema Jenkins & Co., New York.

Pages 128 and 129. *Metropolitan*, 2019, oil on canvas, 60" × 94 ¾". Courtesy of the artist and Sikkema Jenkins & Co., New York.

Page 130. *Riis Beach*, 2019, terra-cotta and manganese oxide wash, 5 ¾" × 6 ¼" × 1 ⅜". Private collection, Italy. Courtesy of the artist and Ciaccia Levi, Paris. Photograph: Aurélien Mole.

Page 131. *Coming Back from the Beach*, 2019, terra-cotta and manganese oxide wash, 15 ¼" × 13 ⅜" × 2 ¾". Private collection, Los Angeles. Courtesy of the artist and Ciaccia Levi, Paris. Photograph: Aurélien Mole.

Page 132. *July*, 2020, oil on canvas, 57" × 38". Courtesy of the artist and Sikkema Jenkins & Co., New York.

Page 133. *Eggs, Dishes, Coreopsis*, 2020, oil on canvas, 42" × 42". Courtesy of the artist and Sikkema Jenkins & Co., New York.

Page 134. *Noon*, 2020, oil on canvas, 12" × 9". Courtesy of the artist and Sikkema Jenkins & Co., New York.

Page 135. *Empty Sunny Room*, 2018, oil and crayon on canvas, 12" × 9". Private collection, Paris. Courtesy of the artist and Ciaccia Levi, Paris. Photograph: Aurélien Mole.

Page 136. *Peonies from Tom, Sword Lilies from Patrice*, 2019, oil on canvas, 12" × 9". Courtesy of the artist and Sikkema Jenkins & Co., New York.

Page 137. *Dance in Shower*, 2019, terra-cotta and manganese oxide wash, 9 ⅝" × 3 ⅛" × 3 ½". Private collection, London. Courtesy of the artist and Ciaccia Levi, Paris. Photograph: Aurélien Mole.

DOUBLE-TALK

GREG MULCAHY

He thought maybe to go out there, to that tiny prairie cemetery some golden afternoon, and leave a flower or a can of some old style label now all contract brewed.

Flower.

Can.

Or both.

Now past understanding.

Concepts empty as a cave.

Some caves are full.

Things he thought the world was or they were part of the world.

And what light, what growth, what order and upkeep in the improbable scene?

DAY

GREG MULCAHY

He sat there like it was a sheathed dagger day.

Or fortune would fall fortunate from the sky.

HEAVEN

GREG MULCAHY

Concerns like things disappeared.

The rest just a story he couldn't be rid of.

I AM A LITTLE WORLD

NATHAN DRAGON

Sometime just after I moved here, on the tiniest Monday, it seemed like something new was low-risk.

I started to take my coffee in a new way, with half-and-half and grade A maple syrup. I wanted to change things up.

I think somebody said that maple syrup is brain food.

I used to take my coffee strong and plain and today a golden rain falls in globs like applesauce.

And when it's warm and sunny we all love the ice cream they sell here.

I am thinking that I am the god of rising air, low pressure, fresh clouds, cyclical weather systems. I get strength from thinking this.

You ever feel like someone who you've seen around a lot but never met is a good friend?—or even someone you fucking hate, like they've been messing with you?

I am that one.

THANKSGIVING

ROBERT TINDALL

Speen puts the doubt and the fear aside. Life is good and he refuses to drink.

The boss where Speen had held a job earlier—Speen seemed to admire. Speen felt good, had no grudges.

Then he had taken a trip to New York City, which was a place that fulfilled every idea of his. People flattered him nor did they mean anything wrong. His youth was done. The traffic was heavy. So he knew some parts of town, the restaurants and the park.

At the saloon Speen had a glass of soda pop—he was happy. Speen liked to remember and he could proceed without much question. The bartender was Spanish, of medium build.

Speen had had a drug habit in college, which did cast a

shadow of doubt on everything he knew about.

Once Speen was back in Chicago he figured the worst was over. The buildings, some of them in the neighborhood, described a morality that told of his life in the town.

The next holiday was Thanksgiving. That was momentum. The calendar year was without much heavy-handedness on anyone's part. The suspense was something new.

Henrietta dropped Speen a line. He was puzzled as to how she had gotten his latest address. He was resigned to being alone, and the future was an opaque thing. Only he would not drink.

A discomfiture also lurked. He sensed Henrietta was laughing at him from a distance. As well, that was nothing new.

The payoff was that things changed undeniably. Henrietta called from the hotel and it seemed they were an item.

The desk clerk handed Speen the keys to the room and he went up the elevator—the place was a beauty. The room was neat, was old-fashioned, with a window over the street and with a toilet off to one side through a door. Speen might have had a false moment now and then, but Henrietta did tolerate him for that and they did make a couple, thereby.

As well, he had forgotten his friend Mick Brenlan, but maybe that would be resurrected.

Along with buses and trains, food and coffee were expensive. The government was paying for the food so maybe that was a free ride. He would go here and there unimpeded and there was plenty of coffee.

He had pleasant memories and the reality was off to the side.

CONTRIBUTORS

Dave Barrett is a poet and short-fiction writer. He lives in St. Francis, Wisconsin.

Kayla Blatchley is a writer and teacher living in Syracuse, New York. Her stories have also appeared in *A Public Space* and online at *Hobart*, *Vol. 1 Brooklyn*, and *New York Tyrant*. She is currently at work on a novel.

Kim Chinquee's seventh collection, *Snowdog*, was published in 2021 with Ravenna Press. Her collection *Pipette* will be published in 2022, also with Ravenna Press, as well as her novel-in-flashes, *Battle Dress*, with Widow + Orphan House. She codirects the writing major at SUNY Buffalo State.

Hedgie Choi received her MFA from the Michener Center. She lives in Baltimore.

Lydia Davis's two most recent nonfiction titles are *Essays One*, on reading, writing, memory, the visual arts, and the Bible (Farrar, Straus and Giroux, 2019), and *Essays Two*, on Proust, translation, and learning languages (FSG, 2021). Her most recent collection of short fiction is *Can't and Won't* (FSG, 2014). Her collection of translations from the Dutch of A. L. Snijders's very short stories, *Night Train*, was published by New Directions in 2021.

Wendy Doniger is the Mircea Eliade Distinguished Service Professor of the History of Religions at the University of Chicago, now Emerita, and the author of over forty books, including *The Hindus:*

An Alternative History (2010), *Hinduism* in the Norton Anthology of World Religions (2014), *The Ring of Truth: And Other Myths of Sex and Jewelry* (2017), *Against Dharma* (2018), *The Donigers of Great Neck: A Mythologized Memoir* (2019), and *Winged Stallions and Wicked Mares: Horses in Indian Myth and History* (2021). In press is a translation of the last books of the *Mahabharata* and in progress is *Letters from India, 1963–2018*.

Nathan Dragon's work has also appeared in *Hotel*, *Fence*, *Sleepingfish*, and *New York Tyrant*.

Carol Edelstein's third book of poems, *Past Repair* (2020), is available from Simian Press.

Lucie Elven is the author of *The Weak Spot*. She lives in London.

The work of Louis Fratino has been the subject of numerous exhibitions, including at Ciaccia Levi, Paris, 2021; Sikkema Jenkins & Co., New York, 2020; Jeff Bailey Gallery, Hudson, New York, 2018; the FLAG Art Foundation, New York, 2019; the National Arts Club, New York, 2019; MAN_Museo d'Arte Provincia di Nuoro, Nuoro, Italy, 2018; and Cabinet Printemps, Düsseldorf, 2018. Fratino's work will be included in upcoming group exhibitions at the Columbus Museum of Art (2021); the RISD Museum, Providence; and Grinnell College Museum of Art. He is a recipient of a Fulbright Research Fellowship in Painting and a Yale Norfolk Painting Fellowship. Fratino lives and works in Brooklyn.

Julie Green (1961–2021) was a recipient of a Joan Mitchell Foundation Painters and Sculptors Grant. Her series *Fashion Plate* will be shown in the spring of 2022 at Elizabeth Houston Gallery in New York. A previous series, *The Last Supper*, illustrates one thousand final meal requests of US death row inmates. Green lived in Oregon.

Augusta Gross composes music for piano and other instruments. Several of her works are featured in pianist Bruce Levingston's albums *Citizen* and *Still Sound*, Janice Friedman's *Below Sea Level* and *In Close Proximity*, and Seunghee Lee and Katrine Gislinge's *Full Circle*.

Mark Hage's photography book *Capital* was published in 2020 by A Public Space Books. He contributed the text for *The Book of Errors*, a visual reimagination of three historic landmarks, and is at work on a collection of stories.

Jonathan Johnson's work has appeared in a variety of journals, including *Necessary Fiction*, *NANO Fiction*, *Dead Reckonings*, *Corium Magazine*, and the *Weird Fiction Review*. He is a senior sales leader for an international engineering firm. He lives in Wisconsin.

Vijay Khurana is a fiction writer and translator from German. He won the 2021 *Griffith Review* Emerging Voices Competition, and his stories have been shortlisted for the Bristol Short Story Prize, the Galley Beggar Press Short Story Prize, and the Cúirt New Writing Prize, among other awards.

Jae Kim is a writer and a literary translator. He holds an MFA in fiction from Washington University in St. Louis, and his translations have received support from the National Endowment for the Arts. His work appears in journals such as *Conjunctions*, *Poetry*, and *Granta*. He currently lives in Tulsa as a Tulsa Artist Fellow.

Darrell Kinsey lives in Watkinsville, Georgia.

Brigitte Lacombe's portraits of many of the world's most celebrated artists, actors, politicians, and intellectuals have been exhibited internationally and featured extensively in magazines during the last four decades. The 2019 documentary film *Brigitte* directed by Lynne Ramsay, commissioned by Miu Miu Women's Tales, was shown at the Venice and New York Film Festivals. Her monographs include *LacombeAnima/Persona* (Steidl/Dangin, 2008) and *Lacombe Cinema/Theater* (Schirmer/Mosel, 2001).

Susan Laier writes both fiction and poetry. Her work has been featured in *Tammy* and *Catapult*. Most recently, her stories have appeared in *MumberMag* and *Linea*. She paints and is a master leather artisan. She lives in Stephentown, New York.

Clancy Martin's new book, on suicide and failing at suicide, is forthcoming from Pantheon in 2022.

Cullen McAndrews lives and works in New York. This is his first published fiction.

Greg Mulcahy is the author of *Out of Work*, *Constellation*, *Carbine*, and *O'Hearn*. He teaches at Century College.

Vi Khi Nao's work includes poetry, fiction, film, theater, and cross-genre collaboration. She was a fall 2019 fellow at the Black Mountain Institute.

Kathryn Scanlan is the author of *Aug 9—Fog* and *The Dominant Animal*. Her third book, *Kick the Latch*, is forthcoming from New Directions in 2022. She lives in Los Angeles.

Christine Schutt's books include the story collections *A Day, a Night, Another Day, Summer* and *Nightwork*. She is the recipient of the 2020 Katherine Anne Porter Award from the American Academy of Arts and Letters. Her novel *All Souls* will appear in translation in Italian in 2022 from Playground, an imprint of Fandango.

Dorothea Tanning (1910–2012) produced over four hundred paintings, drawings, prints, and sculptures. Her work has been acquired by museums nationally and worldwide. Recently her work was exhibited at the Whitney Museum of American Art. She published two memoirs and a novel. Two collections of her poetry appeared just before her death.

Tanning's painting on page 94 is titled *A Family Portrait* © Artists Rights Society (ARS), New York / ADAGP, Paris.

Robert Tindall lives in Evanston, Illinois.

Marc Tweed is a fiction writer and painter living in Seattle. His short stories have appeared in *Cleaver Magazine*, *Juked*, the *Normal School*, and many other publications. He is writing a novel.

Deb Olin Unferth is the author of six books, most recently *Barn 8*.

THE EDITORS WISH TO THANK THE FOLLOWING
FOR THEIR GENEROUS SUPPORT OF NOON:

Eleanor Alper
Katie Baldwin
The Balsamo Family Foundation
Margaret Barrett
Francis and Prudence Beidler
Marcy Brownson and Edwin J. Wesely
Melinda Davis and Ealan Wingate
Lawrie Dean
Eugen Friedlaender Foundation
Nancy Evans
Joseph Glossberg
Lisa Grunwald
Mark Hage
Diane Holsenbeck
Ellen Kern
Christina Kirk
Laura S. Kirk
Lucy Kissel
Lucy and Kenneth Lehman
Shoshanna Lonstein
Joyce Lowinson
Ruth and Irving Malin
Clancy Martin
Pam Michaelcheck
Wolfgang Neumann
Melanie Niemiec
Nuveen Investments
Mary Frances Sears
Szilvia Szmuk-Tanenbaum
Lisa Taylor
Souvankham Thammavongsa
Lily Tuck
Abby S. Weintraub
Paul C. Williams
Anonymous (3)

A NOTE ON THE TYPE

This book was set in Fournier, a typeface named for Pierre Simon Fournier, a celebrated type designer in eighteenth-century France. Fournier's type is considered transitional in that it drew its inspiration from the old style yet was ingeniously innovative, providing for an elegant yet legible appearance. For some time after his death, in 1768, Fournier was remembered primarily as the author of a famous manual of typography and as a pioneer of the print system. However, in 1925 his reputation was enhanced when the Monotype Corporation of London revived Fournier's roman and italic.

Typeset by Will Augerot, Brooklyn, New York
Visual production by Robert Irish
Printed by GHP, West Haven, Connecticut
Cover design by Susan Carroll
NOON is printed on recycled paper
with environmentally friendly inks.

The CENTER *for* FICTION

Writers Studio

Open 8am-10pm, 7 Days a Week • Keycard Access to Building

15 Lafayette Avenue, Brooklyn, New York 11217

Apply at **centerforfiction.org/write**

conjunctions.com

CONJUNCTIONS

biannual print and e-book volumes

weekly online magazine

Edited by Bradford Morrow. Published by Bard College.

"Kim Chinquee writes with remarkable heart and grace."
–Garielle Lutz, author of *The Complete Gary Lutz* and *Worsted*

PIPETTE

Kim Chinquee

Stories

"We wear lab coats, masks and gloves. We pipette.
We hear the hum of the machines."

Ravenna Press | SPRING 2022

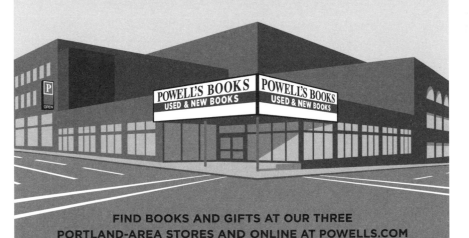

A PUBLIC SPACE

LITERARY AND ARTS MAGAZINE

"A gorgeously curated collection we experience as a cabinet of wonders."
—Whiting Literary Magazine Prize

THE COMMUNICATING VESSELS
FRIEDERIKE MAYRÖCKER

translated by Alexander Booth

"There are very few writers who will truly change the way you approach reading and writing... You, Friederike Mayröcker, have been one of them." —Alexander Booth

CAPITAL
MARK HAGE

photography and essay

"Exquisite." —Ron Slate

"If I were teaching painting, I would use *Capital* as a textbook." —Anne Elliott

GEOMETRY OF SHADOWS
GIORGIO DE CHIRICO

translated by Stefania Heim

The first comprehensive collection of the painter's Italian poems. "As essential and as mysterious as his paintings."
—Jhumpa Lahiri

MAGAZINE · BOOKS · ACADEMY · APS TOGETHER · FELLOWSHIPS

The Corner Bookstore

1313 Madison Avenue at 93rd Street, New York City, 10128

Phone (212) 831-3554 • E-mail info@cornerbookstorenyc.com

www.cornerbookstorenyc.com